AUTUMN SONG
Selected Poems

POETRY FROM CRESCENT MOON

Walking In Cornwall
by Ursula Le Guin

Hymns To the Night
by Novalis

Hymns To the Night: In Translation
by Novalis

Flower Pollen: Selected Thoughts
by Novalis

Novalis: His Life, Thoughts and Works
by Novalis

Edmund Spenser: *Heavenly Love: Selected Poems*
selected and introduced by Teresa Page

Edmund Spenser: *Amoretti*
edited by Teresa Page

The Visions of Petrarch and Bellay: Early Sonnets
by Edmund Spenser

Robert Herrick: *Delight In Disorder: Selected Poems*
edited and introduced by M.K. Pace

Robert Herrick: *Hesperides*
edited and introduced by M.K. Pace

Robert Herrick: *Upon Julia's Breasts: Love Poems*
edited and introduced by M.K. Pace

Sir Thomas Wyatt: *Love For Love: Selected Poems*
selected and introduced by Louise Cooper

John Donne: *Air and Angels: Selected Poems*
selected and introduced by A.H. Ninham

D.H. Lawrence: *Being Alive: Selected Poems*
edited with an introduction by Margaret Elvy

D.H. Lawrence: *Amores*
edited with an introduction by Margaret Elvy

D.H. Lawrence: *Look! We Have Come Through!*
edited with an introduction by Margaret Elvy

D.H. Lawrence: *Love Poems and Others*
edited with an introduction by Margaret Elvy

D.H. Lawrence: *New Poems*
edited with an introduction by Margaret Elvy

D.H. Lawrence: Symbolic Landscapes
by Jane Foster

D.H. Lawrence: Infinite Sensual Violence
by M.K. Pace

Percy Bysshe Shelley: *Paradise of Golden Lights: Selected Poems*
selected and introduced by Charlotte Greene

Thomas Hardy: *Her Haunting Ground: Selected Poems*
edited, with an introduction by A.H. Ninham

Thomas Hardy: *Late Lyrics and Earlier*
edited, with an introduction by A.H. Ninham

Thomas Hardy: *Moments of Vision*
edited, with an introduction by A.H. Ninham

Thomas Hardy: *Poems of the Past and the Present*
edited, with an introduction by A.H. Ninham

Thomas Hardy: *Satires of Circumstance*
edited, with an introduction by A.H. Ninham

Thomas Hardy: *Time's Laughingstocks*
edited, with an introduction by A.H. Ninham

Thomas Hardy: *Wessex Poems*
edited, with an introduction by A.H. Ninham

Sexing Hardy: Thomas Hardy and Feminism
by Margaret Elvy

Emily Bronte: *Darkness and Glory: Selected Poems*
selected and introduced by Miriam Chalk

John Keats: *Bright Star: Selected Poems*
edited with an introduction by Miriam Chalk

John Keats: *Poems of 1820*
edited with an introduction by Miriam Chalk

Henry Vaughan: *A Great Ring of Pure and Endless Light: Selected Poems*
selected and introduced by A.H. Ninham

The Crescent Moon Book of Love Poetry
edited by Louise Cooper

The Crescent Moon Book of Mystical Poetry in English
edited by Carol Appleby

The Crescent Moon Book of Nature Poetry From Langland to Lawrence
edited by Margaret Elvy

The Crescent Moon Book of Metaphysical Poetry
edited and introduced by Charlotte Greene

The Crescent Moon Book of Elizabethan Love Poetry
edited and introduced by Carol Appleby

The Crescent Moon Book of Romantic Poetry
edited and introduced by L.M. Poole

Brigitte's Blue Heart
by Jeremy Reed

Claudia Schiffer's Red Shoes
by Jeremy Reed

By-Blows: Uncollected Poems
by D.J. Enright

Peter Redgrove: Here Comes the Flood
by Jeremy Mark Robinson

Sex-Magic-Poetry-Cornwall: A Flood of Poems
by Peter Redgrove, edited with an essay by Jeremy Mark Robinson

The Troubadours
by H.J. Chaytor

Petrarch, Dante and the Troubadours: The Religion of Love and Poetry
by Cassidy Hughes

Fifteen Sonnets of Petrarch
by Francesco Petrarch
Canzoniere
by Francesco Petrarch

Dante: *Selections From the Vita Nuova*
translated by Thomas Okey

Dante: *Vita Nuova*
translated by Dante Gabriel Rossetti

Dante: *De Monarchia*
translated by F.J. Church

Dante: His Times and His Work
by Arthur John Butler

Arthur Rimbaud: *Selected Poems*
edited and translated by Andrew Jary

Arthur Rimbaud: *A Season in Hell*
edited and translated by Andrew Jary

Friedrich Hölderlin: *Hölderlin's Songs of Light: Selected Poems*
translated by Michael Hamburger

Rainer Maria Rilke: *Dance the Orange: Selected Poems*
translated by Michael Hamburger

Rainer Maria Rilke: *Poems*
translated by Jessie Lamont

Auguste Rodin
by Rainer Maria Rilke

Rilke: Space, Essence and Angels In the Poetry of Rainer Maria Rilke
by B.D. Barnacle

German Romantic Poetry: Goethe, Novalis, Heine, Hölderlin
by Carol Appleby

The North Sea
by Heinrich Heine

Rampoli: Poems From Mainly German
by George Macdonald

Arseny Tarkovsky: *Life, Life: Selected Poems*
translated by Virginia Rounding

Emily Dickinson: *Wild Nights: Selected Poems*
selected and introduced by Miriam Chalk

Diana
by Henry Constable

Delia
by Samuel Daniel

Idea
by Michael Drayton

Astrophil and Stella
by Sir Philip Sidney

Selected Poems
by William Shakespeare

Elizabethan Sonnet Cycles
by Daniel, Drayton, Sidney,
Spenser and Shakespeare

Elizabethan Sonnet Cycles (Volume Two)
by Lodge, Griffin, Smith,
Constable and Fletcher

Three Metaphysical Poets
edited by A.H. Ninham

Three Romantic Poets
edited by Miriam Chalk

AUTUMN SONG

SELECTED POEMS

PAUL VERLAINE

Translated by Arthur Symons
Edited and Introduced by Andrew Jary

CRESCENT MOON

First published 1919. This edition 2021.
© Andrew Jary 2021.

Designed by Radiance Graphics.
Set in Book Antiqua 10 on 14 point.

The right of Andrew Jary to be identified as the editor of *Languorous Ecstasy: Selected Poems* has been asserted generally in accordance with sections 77 and 78 of the Copyright, Designs and Patents Act 1988.

All rights reserved. No part of this book may be reprinted or reproduced, stored in a retrieval system, or transmitted, in any form or by any means, electronic, mechanical, photocopying, recording or otherwise, without permission from the publisher.

British Library Cataloguing in Publication data

Verlaine, Paul
Selected Poems. – (European Poets Series)
I. Title II. Symons, Arthur III. Jary, Andrew IV. Series
841.8

ISBN-13 9781861718075
ISBN-13 9781861718280

CRESCENT MOON PUBLISHING
P.O. Box 1312, Maidstone
Kent, ME14 5XU
Great Britain
www.crmoon.com

Contents

A Note On Texts ✤ 11

CLAIR DE LUNE ✤ 16
PANTOMIME ✤ 18
SUR L'HERBE ✤ 20
L'ALLÉE ✤ 22
À LA PROMENADE ✤ 24
DANS LA GROTTE ✤ 26
LES INGÉNUS ✤ 28
CORTÈGE ✤ 30
LES COQUILLAGES ✤ 32
EN PATINANT ✤ 34
FANTOCHES ✤ 40
CYTHÈRE ✤ 42
EN BATEAU ✤ 44
LE FAUNE ✤ 46
MANDOLINE ✤ 48
A CLYMÈNE ✤ 50
LETTRE ✤ 52
LES INDOLENTS ✤ 56
COLOMBINE ✤ 58
L'AMOUR PAR TERRE ✤ 62

EN SOURDINE ✶ 64
COLLOQUE SENTIMENTAL ✶ 66
SOLEILS COUCHANTS ✶ 68
CHANSON D'AUTOMNE ✶ 70
FEMME ET CHATTE ✶ 72
"LA LUNE BLANCHE" ✶ 74
"LE FOYER" ✶ 76
"C'EST L'EXTASE LANGUOUREUSE" ✶ 78
"JE DIVINE, À TRAVERS UN MURMURE" ✶ 80
"IL PLEURE DANS MON COEUR" ✶ 82
"LE PIANO QUE BAISE UNE MAIN FRELE" ✶ 84
"O TRISTE, TRISTE ÉTAIT MON AME" ✶ 86
"DANS L'INTERMINABLE ENNUI" ✶ 88
"LA FUITE EST VERDATRE ET ROSE" 90
SPLEEN ✶ 92
STREETS ✶ 94
ART POÉTIQUE ✶ 96
MEZZETIN, CHANTANT ✶ 100
"LES CHÈRES MAINS QUI FURENT MIENNES" ✶ 102
"O MON DIEU" ✶ 104
"UN GRAND SOMMEIL NOIR" ✶ 108
"LA TRISTESSE" ✶ 110
"LA MER EST PLUS BELLE" ✶ 112
IMPRESSION FAUSSE ✶ 114
"TU CROIS AU MARC DE CAFÉ" ✶ 116
"WHEN WE GO TOGETHER" ✶ 118

    Paul Verlaine ✶ 124
    A Note on Paul Verlaine ✶ 147
    Bibliography ✶ 153

NOTE ON THE TEXT

The text is from *The Symbolist Movement In Literature* by Arthur Symons, published by E.P. Dutton, New York, 1919.

In French from *Oeuvres Complètes de Paul Verlaine,* published by Vanier, Paris, 1902.

Jean Frédéric Bazille, Paul Verlaine, 1868

Paul Verlaine by Eugène Carrière

AUTUMN SONG
Selected Poems

Fêtes Galantes

CLAIR DE LUNE

Votre âme est un paysage choisi
Que vont charmants masques et bergamasques,
Jouant du luth et dansant et quasi
Tristes sous leurs déguisements fantasques.

Tout en chantant sur le mode mineur
L'amour vainqueur et la vie opportune,
Ils n'ont pas l'air de croire à leur bonheur
Et leur chanson se mêle au clair de lune,

Au calme clair de lune triste et beau,
Qui fait rêver les oiseaux dans les arbres
Et sangloter d'extase les jets d'eau,
Les grands jets d'eau sveltes parmi les marbres.

CLAIR DE LUNE

Your soul is a sealed garden, and there go
With masque and bergamasque fair companies
Playing on lutes and dancing and as though
Sad under their fantastic fripperies.

Though they in minor keys go carolling
Of love the conqueror and of life the boon
They seem to doubt the happiness they sing
And the song melts into the light of the moon,

The sad light of the moon, so lovely fair
That all the birds dream in the leafy shade
And the slim fountains sob into the air
Among the marble statues in the glade.

PANTOMIME

Pierrot, qui n'a rien d'un Clitandre,
Vide un flacon sans plus attendre,
Et, pratique, entame un pâté.

Cassandre, au fond de l'avenue,
Verse une larme méconnue
Sur son neveu déshérité.

Ce faquin d'Arlequin combine
L'enlèvement de Colombine
Et pirouette quatre fois.

Colombine rêve, surprise
De sentir un coeur dans la brise
Et d'entendre en son coeur des voix.

PANTOMIME

Pierrot, no sentimental swain,
Washes a paté down again
With furtive flagons, white and red.

Cassandre, with demure content,
Greets with a tear of sentiment
His nephew disinherited.

That blackguard of a Harlequin
Pirouettes, and plots to win
His Columbine that flits and flies.

Columbine dreams, and starts to find
A sad heart sighing in the wind,
And in her heart a voice that sighs.

SUR L'HERBE

L'abbé divague. – Et toi, marquis,
Tu mets de travers ta perruque.
– Ce vieux vin de Chypre est exquis
Moins, Camargo, que votre nuque.

– Ma flamme… – Do, mi, sol, la, si.
– L'abbé, ta noirceur se dévoile.
– Que je meure, Mesdames, si
Je ne vous décroche une étoile.

– Je voudrais être petit chien!
– Embrassons nos bergères, l'une
Après l'autre. – Messieurs, eh bien?
– Do, mi, sol. – Hé! bonsoir la Lune!

SUR L'HERBE

The Abbé wanders. – Marquis, now
Set straight your periwig, and speak!
 – This Cyprus wine is heavenly, how
Much less, Camargo, than your cheek!

 – My goddess … – Do, mi, sol, la, si.
 – Abbé, such treason who'll forgive you?
 – May I die, ladies, if there be
A star in heaven I will not give you!

 – I'd be my lady's lapdog; then …
 – Shepherdess, kiss your shepherd soon,
Shepherd, come kiss … – Well, gentlemen?
 – Do, mi, so. – Hey, good-night, good moon!

L'ALLÉE

Fardée et peinte comme au temps des bergeries,
Frêle parmi les noeuds énormes de rubans,
Elle passe, sous les ramures assombries,
Dans l'allée où verdit la mousse des vieux bancs,
Avec mille façons et mille afféteries
Qu'on garde d'ordinaire aux perruches chéries.
Sa longue robe à queue est bleue, et l'éventail
Qu'elle froisse en ses doigts fluets aux larges bagues
S'égaie en des sujets érotiques, si vagues
Qu'elle sourit, tout en rêvant, à maint détail.
– Blonde en somme. Le nez mignon avec la bouche
Incarnadine, grasse, et divine d'orgueil
Inconscient. – D'ailleurs plus fine que la mouche
Qui ravive l'éclat un peu niais de l'oeil.

L'ALLÉE

As in the age of shepherd king and queen,
Painted and frail amid her nodding bows,
Under the sombre branches and between
The green and mossy garden-ways she goes,
With little mincing airs one keeps to pet
A darling and provoking perroquet.
Her long-trained robe is blue, the fan she holds
With fluent fingers girt with heavy rings,
So vaguely hints of vague erotic things
That her eye smiles, musing among its folds.
 – Blonde too, a tiny nose, a rosy mouth,
Artful as that sly patch that makes more sly,
In her divine unconscious pride of youth,
The slightly simpering sparkle of the eye.

À LA PROMENADE

Le ciel si pâle et les arbres si grêles
Semblent sourire à nos costumes clairs
Qui vont flottant légers avec des airs
De nonchalance et des mouvements d'ailes.

Et le vent doux ride l'humble bassin,
Et la lueur du soleil qu'atténue
L'ombre des bas tilleuls de l'avenue
Nous parvient bleue et mourante à dessein.

Trompeurs exquis et coquettes charmantes
Coeurs tendres mais affranchis du serment
Nous devisons délicieusement,
Et les amants lutinent les amantes

De qui la main imperceptible sait
Parfois donner un soufflet qu'on échange
Contre un baiser sur l'extrême phalange
Du petit doigt, et comme la chose est

Immensément excessive et farouche,
On est puni par un regard très sec,
Lequel contraste, au demeurant, avec
La moue assez clémente de la bouche.

A LA PROMENADE

The sky so pale, and the trees, such frail things,
Seem as if smiling on our bright array
That flits so light and gay upon the way
With indolent airs and fluttering as of wings.

The fountain wrinkles under a faint wind,
And all the sifted sunlight falling through
The lime-trees of the shadowy avenue
Comes to us blue and shadowy-pale and thinned.

Faultlessly fickle, and yet fond enough,
With fonds hearts not too tender to be free,
We wander whispering deliciously,
And every lover leads a lady-love,

Whose imperceptible and roguish hand
Darts now and then a dainty tap, the lip
Revenges on an extreme finger-tip,
The tip of the left little finger, and,

The deed being so excessive and uncouth,
A duly freezing look deals punishment,
That in the instant of the act is blent
With a shy pity pouting in the mouth.

DANS LA GROTTE

Là, je me tue à vos genoux!
Car ma détresse est infinie,
Et la tigresse épouvantable d'Hyrcanie
Est une agnelle au prix de vous.

Oui, céans, cruelle Clymène,
Ce glaive qui, dans maints combats,
Mit tant de Scipions et de Cyrus à bas,
Va finir ma vie et ma peine!

Ai-je même besoin de lui
Pour descendre aux Champs-Elysées?
Amour perça-t-il pas de flèches aiguisées
Mon coeur, dès que votre oeil m'eût lui?

DANS LA GROTTE

Stay, let me die, since I am true,
For my distress will not delay,
And the Hyrcanian tigress ravening for prey
Is as a little lamb to you.

Yes, here within, cruel Clymène,
This steel which in how many wars
How many a Cyrus slew, or Scipio, now prepares
To end my life and end my pain.

But nay, what need of steel have I
To haste my passage to the shades?
Did not Love pierce my heart, beyond all mortal aids,
With the first arrow of your eye?

LES INGÉNUS

Les hauts talons luttaient avec les longues jupes,
En sorte que, selon le terrain et le vent,
Parfois luisaient des bas de jambe, trop souvent
Interceptés! – et nous aimions ce jeu de dupes.

Parfois aussi le dard d'un insecte jaloux
Inquiétait le col des belles, sous les branches,
Et c'était des éclairs soudains de nuques blanches
Et ce régal comblait nos jeunes yeux de fous.

Le soir tombait, un soir équivoque d'automne:
Les belles, se pendant rêveuses à nos bras,
Dirent alors des mots si spécieux, tout bas,
Que notre âme depuis ce temps tremble et s'étonne.

LES INGENUS

High heels and long skirts intercepting them,
So that, according to the wind or way,
An ankle peeped and vanished as in play;
And well we loved the malice of the game.

Sometimes an insect with its jealous sting
Some fair one's whiter neck disquieted,
From which the gleams of sudden whiteness shed
Met in our eyes a frolic welcoming.

The stealthy autumn evening faded out,
And the fair creatures dreaming by our side
Words of such subtle savour to us sighed
That since that time our souls tremble and doubt.

CORTÈGE

Un singe en veste de brocart
Trotte et gambade devant elle
Qui froisse un mouchoir de dentelle
Dans sa main gantée avec art,

Tandis qu'un négrillon tout rouge
Maintient à tour de bras les pans
De sa lourde robe en suspens,
Attentif à tout pli qui bouge ;

Le singe ne perd pas des yeux
La gorge blanche de la dame.
Opulent trésor que réclame
Le torse nu de l'un des dieux ;

Le négrillon parfois soulève
Plus haut qu'il ne faut, l'aigrefin,
Son fardeau somptueux, afin
De voir ce dont la nuit il rêve ;

Elle va par les escaliers,
Et ne paraît pas davantage
Sensible à l'insolent suffrage
De ses animaux familiers.

CORTÈGE

A silver-vested monkey trips
And pirouettes before the face
Of one who twists a kerchief's lace
Between her well-gloved finger-tips.

A little negro, a red elf,
Carries her dropping train, and holds
At arm's length all the heavy folds,
Watching each fold displace itself.

The monkey never lets his eyes
Wander from the fair woman's breast,
White wonder that to be possessed
Would call a god out of the skies.

Sometimes the little negro seems
To lift his sumptuous burden up
Higher than need be, in the hope
Of seeing what all night he dreams.

She goes by corridor and stair,
Still to the insolent appeals
Of her familiar animals
Indifferent or unaware.

LES COQUILLAGES

Chaque coquillage incrusté
Dans la grotte où nous nous aimâmes
A sa particularité.

L'un a la pourpre de nos âmes
Dérobée au sang de nos coeurs
Quand je brûle et que tu t'enflammes;

Cet autre affecte tes langueurs
Et tes pâleurs alors que, lasse,
Tu m'en veux de mes yeux moqueurs;

Celui-ci contrefait la grâce
De ton oreille, et celui-là
Ta nuque rose, courte et grasse;

Mais un, entre autres, me troubla.

LES COQUILLAGES

Each shell incrusted in the grot
Where we two loved each other well
An aspect of its own has got.

The purple of a purple shell
Is our souls' colour when they make
Our burning heart's blood visible.

This pallid shell affects to take
Thy languors, when thy love-tired eyes
Rebuke me for my mockery's sake.

This counterfeits the harmonies
Of thy pink ear, and this might be
Thy plump short nape with rosy dyes.

But one, among these, troubled me.

EN PATINANT

Nous fûmes dupes, vous et moi,
De manigances mutuelles,
Madame, à cause de l'émoi
Dont l'Été férut nos cervelles.

Le Printemps avait bien un peu
Contribué, si ma mémoire
Est bonne, à brouiller notre jeu,
Mais que d'une façon moins noire!

Car au printemps l'air est si frais
Qu'en somme les roses naissantes,
Qu'Amour semble entr'ouvrir exprès,
Ont des senteurs presque innocentes;

Et même les lilas ont beau
Pousser leur haleine poivrée,
Dans l'ardeur du soleil nouveau,
Cet excitant au plus récrée,

Tant le zéphir souffle, moqueur,
Dispersant l'aphrodisiaque
Effluve, en sorte que le coeur
Chôme et que même l'esprit vaque,

Et qu'émoustillés, les cinq sens
Se mettent alors de la fête,
Mais seuls, tout seuls, bien seuls et sans
Que la crise monte à la tête.

Ce fut le temps, sous de clairs ciels
(Vous en souvenez-vous, Madame?),

Des baisers superficiels
Et des sentiments à fleur d'âme,

Exempts de folles passions,
Pleins d'une bienveillance amène.
Comme tous deux nous jouissions
Sans enthousiasme – et sans peine!

Heureux instants! – mais vint l'Été:
Adieu, rafraîchissantes brises?
Un vent de lourde volupté
Investit nos âmes surprises.

Des fleurs aux calices vermeils
Nous lancèrent leurs odeurs mûres,
Et partout les mauvais conseils
Tombèrent sur nous des ramures

Nous cédâmes à tout cela,
Et ce fut un bien ridicule
Vertigo qui nous affola
Tant que dura la canicule.

Rires oiseux, pleurs sans raisons,
Mains indéfiniment pressées,
Tristesses moites, pâmoisons,
Et quel vague dans les pensées!

L'automne heureusement, avec
Son jour froid et ses bises rudes,
Vint nous corriger, bref et sec,
De nos mauvaises habitudes,

Et nous induisit brusquement
En l'élégance réclamée

De tout irréprochable amant
Comme de toute digne aimée...

Or cet Hiver, Madame, et nos
Parieurs tremblent pour leur bourse,
Et déjà les autres traîneaux
Osent nous disputer la course.

Les deux mains dans votre manchon,
Tenez-vous bien sur la banquette
Et filons! – et bientôt Fanchon
Nous fleurira quoiqu'on caquette!

EN PATINANT

We were the victims, you and I,
Madame, of mutual self deceits;
And that which set our brains awry
May well have been the summer heats.

And the spring too, if I recall,
Contributed to spoil our play,
And yet its share, I think, was small
In leading you and me astray.

For air in springtime is so fresh
That rose-buds Love has surely meant
To match the roses of the flesh
Have odours almost innocent;

And even the lilies that outpour
Their biting odours where the sun
Is new in heaven, do but the more
Enliven and enlighten one,

So stealthily the zephyr blows
A mocking breath that renders back
The heart's rest and the soul's repose
And the flower's aphrodisiac,

And the five senses, peeping out,
Take up their station at the feast,
But, being by themselves, without
Troubling the reason in the least.

That was the time of azure skies,
(Madame, do you remember it?)

And sonnets to my lady's eyes,
And cautious kisses not too sweet.

Free from all passion's idle pother,
Full of mere kindliness, how long,
How well we liked not loved each other,
Without one rapture or one wrong!

Ah, happy hours! But summer came:
Farewell, fresh breezes of the spring!
A wind of pleasure like a flame
Leapt on our senses wondering.

Strange flowers, fair crimson-hearted flowers
Poured their ripe odours over us,
And evil voices of the hours
Whispered above us in the boughs.

We yielded to it all, ah me!
What vertigo of fools held fast
Our senses in its ecstasy
Until the heat of summer passed?

There were vain tears and vainer laughter,
And hands indefinitely pressed,
Moist sadnesses, and swoonings after,
And what vague void within the breast?

But autumn came to our relief,
Its light grown cold, its gusts grown rough,
Came to remind us, sharp and brief,
That we had wantoned long enough,

And led us quickly to recover
The elegance demanded of

Every quite irreproachable lover
And every seemly lady-love.

Now it is winter, and, alas,
Our backers tremble for their stake;
Already other sledges pass
And leave us toiling in their wake.

Put both your hands into your muff,
Sit back, now, steady! off we go.
Fanchon will tell us soon enough
Whatever news there is to know.

FANTOCHES

Scaramouche et Pulcinella,
Qu'un mauvais dessein rassembla,
Gesticulent, noirs sur la lune.

Cependant l'excellent docteur
Bolonais cueille avec lenteur
Des simples parmi l'herbe brune.

Lors sa fille, piquant minois,
Sous la charmille en tapinois
Se glisse demi-nue, en quête

De son beau pirate espagnol,
Dont un langoureux rossignol
Clame la détresse à tue-tête.

FANTOCHES

Scaramouche waves a threatening hand
To Pulcinella, and they stand,
Two shadows, black against the moon.

The old doctor of Bologna pries
For simples with impassive eyes,
And mutters o'er a magic rune.

The while his daughter, scarce half-dressed,
Glides slyly 'neath the trees, in quest
Of her bold pirate lover's sail;

Her pirate from the Spanish main,
Whose passion thrills her in the pain
Of the loud languorous nightingale.

CYTHÈRE

Un pavillon à claires-voies
Abrite doucement nos joies
Qu'éventent des rosiers amis;

L'odeur des roses, faible, grâce
Au vent léger d'été qui passe,
Se mêle aux parfums qu'elle a mis;

Comme ses yeux l'avaient promis,
Son courage est grand et sa lèvre
Communique une exquise fièvre;

Et l'Amour comblant tout, hormis
La Faim, sorbets et confitures
Nous préservent des courbatures.

CYTHÈRE

By favourable breezes fanned,
A trellised harbour is at hand
To shield us from the summer airs;

The scent of roses, fainting sweet,
Afloat upon the summer heat,
Blends with the perfume that she wears.

True to the promise her eyes gave,
She ventures all, and her mouth rains
A dainty fever through my veins;

And, Love fulfilling all things, save
Hunger, we 'scape, with sweets and ices,
The folly of Love's sacrifices.

EN BATEAU

L'étoile du berger tremblote
Dans l'eau plus noire et le pilote
Cherche un briquet dans sa culotte.

C'est l'instant, Messieurs, ou jamais,
D'être audacieux, et je mets
Mes deux mains partout désormais!

Le chevalier Atys qui gratte
Sa guitare, à Chloris l'ingrate
Lance une oeillade scélérate.

L'abbé confesse bas Églé,
Et ce vicomte déréglé
Des champs donne à son coeur la clé.

Cependant la lune se lève
Et l'esquif en sa course brève
File gaîment sur l'eau qui rêve.

EN BATEAU

The shepherd's star with trembling glint
Drops in black water; at the hint
The pilot fumbles for his flint.

Now is the time or never, sirs.
No hand that wanders wisely errs:
I touch a hand, and is it hers?

The knightly Atys strikes the strings,
And to the faithless Chloris flings
A look that speaks of many things.

The abbé has absolved again
Eglé, the viscount all in vain
Has given his hasty heart the rein.

Meanwhile the moon is up and streams
Upon the skiff that flies and seems
To float upon a tide of dreams.

LE FAUNE

Un vieux faune de terre cuite
Rit au centre des boulingrins,
Présageant sans doute une suite
Mauvaise à ces instants sereins

Qui m'ont conduit et t'ont conduite,
Mélancoliques pèlerins,
Jusqu'à cette heure dont la fuite
Tournoie au son des tambourins.

LE FAUNE

An aged faun of old red clay –
Laughs from the grassy bowling-green,
Foretelling doubtless some decay
Of mortal moments so serene

That lead us lightly on our way
(Love's piteous pilgrims have we been!)
To this last hour that runs away
Dancing to the tambourine.

MANDOLINE

Les donneurs de sérénades
Et les belles écouteuses
Échangent des propos fades
Sous les ramures chanteuses.

C'est Tircis et c'est Aminte,
Et c'est l'éternel Clitandre,
Et c'est Damis qui pour mainte
Cruelle fait maint vers tendre.

Leurs courtes vestes de soie,
Leurs longues robes à queues,
Leur élégance, leur joie
Et leurs molles ombres bleues,

Tourbillonnent dans l'extase
D'une lune rose et grise,
Et la mandoline jase
Parmi les frissons de brise.

MANDOLINE

The singers of serenades
Whisper their faded vows
Unto fair listening maids
Under the singing boughs.

Tircis, Aminte, are there,
Clitandre has waited long,
And Damis for many a fair
Tyrant makes many a song.

Their short vests, silken and bright,
Their long pale silken trains,
Their elegance of delight,
Twine soft blue silken chains.

And the mandolines and they,
Faintlier breathing, swoon
Into the rose and grey
Ecstasy of the moon.

A CLYMÈNE

Mystiques barcarolles,
Romances sans paroles,
Chère, puisque tes yeux,
Couleur des cieux,

Puisque ta voix, étrange
Vision qui dérange
Et trouble l'horizon
De ma raison,

Puisque l'arôme insigne
De ta pâleur de cygne
Et puisque la candeur
De ton odeur,

Ah! puisque tout ton être,
Musique qui pénètre,
Nimbes d'anges défunts,
Tons et parfums.

A sur d'almes cadences
En ses correspondances,
Induit mon coeur subtil,
Ainsi soit-il!

A CLYMÈNE

Mystical strains unheard,
A song without a word,
Dearest, because thine eyes,
Pale as the skies,

Because thy voice, remote
As the far clouds that float
Veiling for me the whole
Heaven of the soul,

Because the stately scent
Of thy swan's whiteness, blent
With the white lily's bloom
Of thy perfume,

Ah! because thy dear love,
The music breathed above
By angels halo-crowned,
Odour and sound,

Hath, in my subtle heart,
With some mysterious art
Transposed thy harmony,
So let it be!

LETTRE

Eloigné de vos yeux, Madame, par des soins
Impérieux (j'en prends tous les dieux à témoins),
Je languis et je meurs, comme c'est ma coutume
En pareil cas, et vais, le coeur plein d'amertume,
A travers des soucis où votre ombre me suit,
Le jour dans mes pensées, dans mes rêves la nuit.
Et la nuit et le jour adorable, Madame!
Si bien qu'enfin, mon corps faisant place à mon âme,
Je deviendrai fantôme à mon tour aussi, moi,
Et qu'alors, et parmi le lamentable émoi
Des enlacements vains et des désirs sans nombre,
Mon ombre se fondra à jamais en notre ombre.

En attendant, je suis, très chère, ton valet.

Tout se comporte-t-il là-bas comme il te plaît,
Ta perruche, ton chat, ton chien? La compagnie
Est-elle toujours belle, et cette Silvanie
Dont j'eusse aimé l'oeil noir si le tien n'était bleu,
Et qui parfois me fit des signes, palsambleu!

Te sert-elle toujours de douce confidente?
Or, Madame, un projet impatient me hante
De conquérir le monde et tous ses trésors pour
Mettre à vos pieds ce gage – indigne – d'un amour
Égal à toutes les flammes les plus célèbres
Qui des grands coeurs aient fait resplendir les ténèbres.
Cléopâtre fut moins aimée, oui, sur ma foi!
Par Marc-Antoine et par César que vous par moi,
N'en doutez pas, Madame, et je saurai combattre
Comme César pour un sourire, ô Cléopâtre,
Et comme Antoine fuir au seul prix d'un baiser.

Sur ce, très chère, adieu. Car voilà trop causer
Et le temps que l'on perd à lire une missive
N'aura jamais valu la peine qu'on l'écrive.

LETTRE

Far from your sight removed by thankless cares
(The gods are witness when a lover swears)
I languish and I die, Madame, as still
My use is, which I punctually fulfil,
And go, through heavy-hearted woes conveyed,
Attended ever by your lovely shade,
By day in thought, by night in dreams of hell,
And day and night, Madame, adorable!
So that at length my dwindling body lost
In very soul, I too become a ghost,
I too, and in the lamentable stress
Of vain desires remembering happiness,
Remembered kisses, now, alas, unfelt,
My shadow shall into your shadow melt.

Meanwhile, dearest, your most obedient slave.

How does the sweet society behave,
Thy cat, thy dog, thy parrot? and is she
Still, as of old, the black-eyed Silvanie
(I had loved black eyes if thine had not been blue)
Who ogled me at moments, palsambleu!

Thy tender friend and thy sweet confidant?
One dream there is, Madame, long wont to haunt
This too impatient heart: to pour the earth
And all its treasures (of how little worth!)
Before your feet as tokens of a love
Equal to the most famous flames that move
The hearts of men to conquer all but death.
Cleopatra was less loved, yes, on my faith,
By Antony or Cæsar than you are,

Madame, by me, who truly would by far
Out-do the deeds of Cæsar for a smile,
O Cleopatra, queen of word and wile,
Or, for a kiss, take flight with Antony

With this, farewell, dear, and no more from me;
How can the time it takes to read it, quite
Be worth the trouble that it took to write?

LES INDOLENTS

Bah! malgré les destins jaloux,
Mourons ensemble, voulez-vous?
 – La proposition est rare.

 – Le rare est le bon. Donc mourons
Comme dans les Décamérons.
 – Hi! hi! hi! quel amant bizarre!

 – Bizarre, je ne sais. Amant
Irréprochable, assurément.
Si vous voulez, mourons ensemble?

 – Monsieur, vous raillez mieux encor
Que vous n'aimez, et parlez d'or;
Mais taisons-nous, si bon vous semble?

Si bien que ce soir-là Tircis
Et Dorimène, à deux assis
Non loin de deux silvains hilares,

Eurent l'inexpiable tort
D'ajourner une exquise mort.
Hi! hi! hi! les amants bizarres!

LES INDOLENTS

Bah! spite of Fate, that says us nay,
Suppose we die together, eh?
 – A rare conclusion you discover

 – What's rare is good. Let us die so,
Like lovers in Boccaccio.
 – Ha! ha! ha! you fantastic lover!

 – Nay, not fantastic. If you will,
Fond, surely irreproachable.
Suppose, then, that we die together?

 – Good sir, your jests are fitlier told
Than when you speak of love or gold.
Why speak at all, in this glad weather?

Whereat, behold them once again,
Tircis beside his Dorimène,
Not far from two blithe rustic rovers,

For some caprice of idle breath
Deferring a delicious death.
Ha! ha! ha! what fantastic lovers!

COLOMBINE

Léandre le sot,
Pierrot qui d'un saut
De puce
Franchit le buisson,
Cassandre sous son
Capuce,

Arlequin aussi,
Cet aigrefin si
Fantasque
Aux costumes fous,
Ses yeux luisants sous
Son masque,

 – Do, mi, sol, mi, fa, –
Tout ce monde va,
Rit, chante
Et danse devant
Une belle enfant
Méchante

Dont les yeux pervers
Comme les yeux verts
Des chattes
Gardent ses appas
Et disent: «A bas
Les pattes!»

 – Eux ils vont toujours!
Fatidique cours
Des astres,
Oh! dis-moi vers quels

Mornes ou cruels
Désastres

L'implacable enfant,
Preste et relevant
Ses jupes,
La rose au chapeau,
Conduit son troupeau
De dupes?

COLUMBINE

The foolish Leander,
Cape-covered Cassander,
And which
Is Pierrot? 'tis he
With the hop of a flea
Leaps the ditch;

And Harlequin who
Rehearses anew
His sly task,
With his dress that's a wonder,
And eyes shining under
His mask;

Mi, sol, mi, fa, do!
How gaily they go,
And they sing
And they laugh and they twirl
Round the feet of a girl
Like the Spring,

Whose eyes are as green
As a cat's are, and keen
As its claws,
And her eyes without frown
Bid all new-comers Down
With your paws!

On they go with the force
Of the stars in their course,
And the speed:
O tell me toward what

Disaster unthought,
Without heed

The implacable fair,
A rose in her hair,
Holding up
Her skirts as she runs
Leads this dance of the dunce
And the dupe?

L'AMOUR PAR TERRE

Le vent de l'autre nuit a jeté bas l'Amour
Qui, dans le coin le plus mystérieux du parc,
Souriait en bandant malignement son arc,
Et dont l'aspect nous fit tant songer tout un jour!

Le vent de l'autre nuit l'a jeté bas! Le marbre
Au souffle du matin tournoie, épars. C'est triste
De voir le piédestal, où le nom de l'artiste
Se lit péniblement parmi l'ombre d'un arbre.

Oh! c'est triste de voir debout le piédestal
Tout seul! et des pensers mélancoliques vont
Et viennent dans mon rêve où le chagrin profond
Évoque un avenir solitaire et fatal.

Oh! c'est triste! – Et toi-même, est-ce pas? es touchée
D'un si dolent tableau, bien que ton oeil frivole
S'amuse au papillon de pourpre et d'or qui vole
Au-dessus des débris dont l'allée est jonchée.

L'AMOUR PAR TERRE

The other night a sudden wind laid low
The Love, shooting an arrow at a mark,
In the mysterious corner of the park,
Whose smile disquieted us long ago.

The wind has overthrown him, and above
His scattered dust, how sad it is to spell
The artist's name still faintly visible
Upon the pedestal without its Love,

How sad it is to see the pedestal
Still standing! as in dream I seem to hear
Prophetic voices whisper in my ear
The lonely and despairing end of all.

How sad it is! Why, even you have found
A tear for it, although your frivolous eye
Laughs at the gold and purple butterfly
Poised on the piteous litter on the ground.

EN SOURDINE

Calmes dans le demi-jour
Que les branches hautes font,
Pénétrons bien notre amour
De ce silence profond.

Fondons nos âmes, nos coeurs
Et nos sens extasiés,
Parmi les vagues langueurs
Des pins et des arbousiers.

Ferme tes yeux à demi,
Croise tes bras sur ton sein,
Et de ton coeur endormi
Chasse à jamais tout dessein.

Laissons-nous persuader
Au souffle berceur et doux
Qui vient à tes pieds rider
Les ondes de gazon roux.

Et quand, solennel, le soir
Des chênes noirs tombera,
Voix de notre désespoir,
Le rossignol chantera.

EN SOURDINE

Calm where twilight leaves have stilled
With their shadow light and sound,
Let our silent love be filled
With a silence as profound.

Let our ravished senses blend
Heart and spirit, thine and mine,
With vague languors that descend
From the branches of the pine.

Close thine eyes against the day,
Fold thine arms across thy breast,
And for ever turn away
All desire of all but rest.

Let the lulling breaths that pass
In soft wrinkles at thy feet,
Tossing all the tawny grass,
This and only this repeat.

And when solemn evening
Dims the forest's dusky air,
Then the nightingale shall sing
The delight of our despair.

COLLOQUE SENTIMENTAL

Dans le vieux parc solitaire et glacé
Deux formes ont tout à l'heure passé.

Leurs yeux sont morts et leurs lèvres sont molles,
Et l'on entend à peine leurs paroles.

Dans le vieux parc solitaire et glacé
Deux spectres ont évoqué le passé.

– Te souvient-il de notre extase ancienne?
– Pourquoi voulez-vous donc qu'il m'en souvienne?

– Ton coeur bat-il toujours à mon seul nom?
Toujours vois-tu mon âme en rêve? – Non.

– Ah! les beaux jours de bonheur indicible
Où nous joignions nos bouches! – C'est possible.

Qu'il était bleu, le ciel, et grand l'espoir!
– L'espoir a fui, vaincu, vers le ciel noir.

Tels ils marchaient dans les avoines folles,
Et la nuit seule entendit leurs paroles.

COLLOQUE SENTIMENTAL

In the old park, solitary and vast,
Over the frozen ground two forms once passed.

Their lips were languid and their eyes were dead,
And hardly could be heard the words they said.

In the old park, solitary and vast,
Two ghosts once met to summon up the past.

 – Do you remember our old ecstasy?
 – Why would you bring it back again to me?

 – Do you still dream as you dreamed long ago?
Does your heart beat to my heart's beating?
 – No.

 – Ah, those old days, what joys have those days seen
When your lips met my lips! – It may have been.

 – How blue the sky was, and our hope how light!
 – Hope has flown helpless back into the night.

They walked through weeds withered and grasses dead,
And only the night heard the words they said.

From Poèmes Saturniens

SOLEILS COUCHANTS

Une aube affaiblie
Verse par les champs
La mélancolie
Des soleils couchants.
La mélancolie
Berce de doux chants
Mon coeur qui s'oublie
Aux soleils couchants.
Et d'étranges rêves,
Comme des soleils
Couchants, sur les grèves,
Fantômes vermeils,
Défilent sans trêves,
Défilent, pareils
A des grands soleils
Couchants, sur les grèves.

SOLEILS COUCHANTS

Pale dawn delicately
Over earth has spun
The sad melancholy
Of the setting sun.
Sad melancholy
Brings oblivion
In sad songs to me
With the setting sun.
And the strangest dreams,
Dreams like suns that set
On the banks of the streams,
Ghost and glory met,
To my sense it seems,
Pass, and without let,
Like great suns that set
On the banks of streams.

CHANSON D'AUTOMNE

Les sanglots longs
Des violons
    De l'automne
Blessent mon coeur
D'une langueur
    Monotone.

Tout suffocant
Et blême, quand
    Sonne l'heure,
Je me souviens
Des jours anciens
    Et je pleure;

Et je m'en vais
Au vent mauvais
    Qui m'emporte
Deçà, delà,
Pareil à la
    Feuille morte.

CHANSON D'AUTOMNE

When a sighing begins
In the violins
Of the autumn-song,
My heart is drowned
In the slow sound
Languorous and long.

Pale as with pain,
Breath fails me when
The hour tolls deep.
My thoughts recover
The days that are over,
And I weep.

And I go

Where the winds know,
Broken and brief,
To and fro,
As the winds blow
A dead leaf.

FEMME ET CHATTE

Elle jouait avec sa chatte;
Et c'était merveille de voir
La main blanche et la blanche patte
S'ébattre dans l'ombre du soir.

Elle cachait – la scélérate! –
Sous ces mitaines de fil noir
Ses meurtriers ongles d'agate,
Coupants et clairs comme un rasoir.

L'autre aussi faisait la sucrée
Et rentrait sa griffe acérée,
Mais le diable n'y perdait rien…

Et dans le boudoir où, sonore,
Tintait son rire aérien,
Brillaient quatre points de phosphore.

FEMME ET CHATTE

They were at play, she and her cat,
And it was marvellous to mark
The white paw and the white hand pat
Each other in the deepening dark.

The stealthy little lady hid
Under her mittens' silken sheath
Her deadly agate nails that thrid
The silk-like dagger-points of death.

The cat purred primly and drew in
Her claws that were of steel filed thin:
The devil was in it all the same.

And in the boudoir, while a shout
Of laughter in the air rang out,
Four sparks of phosphor shone like flame.

From La Bonne Chanson

I

La lune blanche
Luit dans les bois;
De chaque branche
Part une voix
Sous la ramée…

O bien-aimée.

L'étang reflète,
Profond miroir,
La silhouette
Du saule noir
Où le vent pleure…

Rêvons, c'est l'heure.

Un vaste et tendre
Apaisement
Semble descendre
Du firmament
Que l'astre irise…

C'est l'heure exquise.

I

The white moon sits
And seems to brood
Where a swift voice flits
From each branch in the wood
That the tree-tops cover....

O lover, my lover!

The pool in the meadows
Like a looking-glass
Casts back the shadows
That over it pass
Of the willow-bower....

Let us dream: 'tis the hour....

A tender and vast
Lull of content
Like a cloud is cast
From the firmament
Where one planet is bright....

'Tis the hour of delight.

II

Le foyer, la lueur étroite de la lampe;
La rêverie avec le doigt contre la tempe
Et les yeux se perdant parmi les yeux aimés;
L'heure du thé fumant et des livres fermés;
La douceur de sentir la fin de la soirée;
La fatigue charmante et l'attente adorée
De l'ombre nuptiale et de la douce nuit,
Oh! tout cela, mon rêve attendri le poursuit
Sans relâche, à travers toutes remises vaines,
Impatient des mois, furieux des semaines!

II

The fireside, the lamp's little narrow light;
The dream with head on hand, and the delight
Of eyes that lose themselves in loving looks;
The hour of steaming tea and of shut books;
The solace to know evening almost gone;
The dainty weariness of waiting on
The nuptial shadow and night's softest bliss;
Ah, it is this that without respite, this
That without stay, my tender fancy seeks,
Mad with the months and furious with the weeks.

From Romances sans Paroles

I

C'est l'extase langoureuse,
C'est la fatigue amoureuse,
C'est tous les frissons des bois
Parmi l'étreinte des brises,
C'est, vers les ramures grises,
Le choeur des petites voix.

O le frêle et frais murmure!
Cela gazouille et susure,
Cela ressemble au cri doux
Que l'herbe agitée expire…
Tu dirais, sous l'eau qui vire,
Le roulis sourd des cailloux.

Cette âme qui se lamente
En cette plainte dormante,
C'est la nôtre, n'est-ce pas?
La mienne, dis, et la tienne,
Dont s'exhale l'humble antienne
Par ce tiède soir, tout bas?

I

'Tis the ecstasy of repose,
'Tis love when tired lids close,
'Tis the wood's long shuddering
In the embrace of the wind,
'Tis, where grey boughs are thinned,
Little voices that sing.

O fresh and frail is the sound
That twitters above, around,
Like the sweet tiny sigh
That lies in the shaken grass;
Or the sound when waters pass
And the pebbles shrink and cry.

What soul is this that complains
Over the sleeping plains,
And what is it that it saith?
Is it mine, is it thine,
This lowly hymn I divine
In the warm night, low as a breath?

II

Je devine, à travers un murmure,
Le contour subtil des voix anciennes
Et dans les lueurs musiciennes,
Amour pâle, une aurore future!

Et mon âme et mon coeur en délires
Ne sont plus qu'une espèce d'oeil double
Où tremblote à travers un jour trouble
L'ariette, hélas! de toutes lyres!

O mourir de cette mort seulette
Que s'en vont, cher amour qui t'épeures
Balançant jeunes et vieilles heures!
O mourir de cette escarpolette!

II

I divine, through the veil of a murmuring,
The subtle contour of voices gone,
And I see, in the glimmering lights that sing,
The promise, pale love, of a future dawn.

And my soul and my heart in trouble
What are they but an eye that sees,
As through a mist an eye sees double,
Airs forgotten of songs like these?

O to die of no other dying,
Love, than this that computes the showers
Of old hours and of new hours flying:
O to die of the swing of the hours!

III

Il pleut doucement sur la ville.
(ARTHUR RAIMBAUD.)

Il pleure dans mon coeur
Comme il pleut sur la ville,
Quelle est cette langueur
Qui pénètre mon coeur?

O bruit doux de la pluie
Par terre et sur les toits!
Pour un coeur qui s'ennuie,
O le chant de la pluie!

Il pleure sans raison
Dans ce coeur qui s'écoeure.
Quoi! nulle trahison?
Ce deuil est sans raison.

C'est bien la pire peine
De ne savoir pourquoi,
Sans amour et sans haine,
Mon coeur a tant de peine!

III

Tears in my heart that weeps,
Like the rain upon the town.
What drowsy languor steeps
In tears my heart that weeps?

O sweet sound of the rain
On earth and on the roofs!
For a heart's weary pain
O the song of the rain!

Vain tears, vain tears, my heart!
What, none hath done thee wrong?
Tears without reason start
From my disheartened heart.

This is the weariest woe,
O heart, of love and hate
Too weary, not to know
Why thou hast all this woe.

IV

Son joyeux, importun d'un clavecin sonore.
(PÉTRUS BOREL.)

Le piano que baise une main frêle
Luit dans le soir rose et gris vaguement,
Tandis qu'avec un très léger bruit d'aile
Un air bien vieux, bien faible et bien charmant,
Rôde discret, épeuré quasiment,
Par le boudoir longtemps parfumé d'Elle.

Qu'est-ce que c'est que ce berceau soudain
Qui lentement dorlotte mon pauvre être?
Que voudrais-tu de moi, doux chant badin?
Qu'as-tu voulu, fin refrain incertain
Qui va tantôt mourir vers la fenêtre
Ouverte un peu sur le petit jardin?

IV

A frail hand in the rose-grey evening
Kisses the shining keys that hardly stir,
While, with the light, small flutter of a wing,
And old song, like an old tired wanderer,
Goes very softly, as if trembling,
About the room long redolent of Her.

What lullaby is this that comes again
To dandle my poor being with its breath?
What wouldst thou have of me, gay laughing strain?
What hadst thou, desultory faint refrain
That now into the garden to thy death
Floatest through the half-opened window-pane?

V

O triste, triste était mon âme
A cause, à cause d'une femme.

Je ne me suis pas consolé
Bien que mon coeur s'en soit allé,

Bien que mon coeur, bien que mon âme
Eussent fui loin de cette femme.

Je ne me suis pas consolé
Bien que mon coeur s'en soit allé.

Et mon coeur, mon coeur trop sensible
Dit à mon âme: Est-il possible,

Est-il possible, – le fût-il, –
Ce fier exil, ce triste exil?

Mon âme dit à mon coeur: Sais-je
Moi-même, que nous veut ce piège

D'être présents bien qu'exilés,
Encore que loin en allés?

V

O sad, sad was my soul, alas!
For a woman, a woman's sake it was.

I have had no comfort since that day,
Although my heart went its way,

Although my heart and my soul went
From the woman into banishment.

I have had no comfort since that day,
Although my heart went its way.

And my heart, being sore in me,
Said to my soul: How can this be,

How can this be or have been thus,
This proud, sad banishment of us?

My soul said to my heart: Do I
Know what snare we are tangled by,

Seeing that, banished, we know not whether
We are divided or together?

VI

Dans l'interminable
Ennui de la plaine,
La neige incertaine
Luit comme du sable.

Le ciel est de cuivre
Sans lueur aucune,
On croirait voir vivre
Et mourir la lune.

Comme des nuées
Flottent gris les chênes
Des forêts prochaines
Parmi les buées.

Le ciel est de cuivre
Sans lueur aucune.
On croirait voir vivre
Et mourir la lune.

Corneille poussive
Et vous les loups maigres,
Par ces bises aigres
Quoi donc vous arrive?

Dans l'interminable
Ennui de la plaine,
La neige incertaine
Luit comme du sable.

VI

Wearily the plain's
Endless length expands;
The snow shines like grains
Of the shifting sands.

Light of day is none,
Brazen is the sky;
Overhead the moon
Seems to live and die.

Where the woods are seen,
Grey the oak-trees lift
Through the vaporous screen
Like the clouds that drift.

Light of day is none,
Brazen is the sky;
Overhead the moon
Seems to live and die.

Broken-winded crow,
And you, lean wolves, when
The sharp north-winds blow,
What do you do then?

Wearily the plain's
Endless length expands;
The snow shines like grains
Of the shifting sands.

VII

La fuite est verdâtre et rose
Des collines et des rampes,
Dans un demi-jour de lampes
Qui vient brouiller toute chose.

L'or sur les humbles abîmes,
Tout doucement s'ensanglante,
Des petits arbres sans cimes,
Où quelque oiseau faible chante.

Triste à peine tant s'effacent
Ces apparences d'automne.
Toutes mes langueurs rêvassent,
Que berce l'air monotone.

VII

There's a flight of green and red
In the hurry of hills and rails,
Through the shadowy twilight shed
By the lamps as daylight pales.

Dim gold light flushes to blood
In humble hollows far down;
Birds sing low from a wood
Of barren trees without crown.

Scarcely more to be felt
Than that autumn is gone;
Languors, lulled in me, melt
In the still air's monotone.

SPLEEN

Les roses étaient toutes rouges,
Et les lierres étaient tout noirs.
Chère, pour peu que tu te bouges,
Renaissent tous mes désespoirs.

Le ciel était trop bleu, trop tendre,
La mer trop verte et l'air trop doux.
Je crains toujours, – ce qu'est d'attendre
Quelque fuite atroce de vous.

Du houx à la feuille vernie
Et du luisant buis je suis las,
Et de la campagne infinie
Et de tout, fors de vous, hélas!

SPLEEN

The roses were all red,
The ivy was all black:
Dear, if you turn your head,
All my despairs come back.

The sky was too blue, too kind,
The sea too green, and the air
Too calm: and I know in my mind
I shall wake and not find you there.

I am tired of the box-tree's shine
And the holly's, that never will pass,
And the plain's unending line,
And of all but you, alas!

STREETS

Dansons la gigue!

J'aimais surtout ses jolis yeux,
Plus clairs que l'étoile des cieux,
J'aimais ses yeux malicieux.

Dansons la gigue!

Elle avait des façons vraiment
De désoler un pauvre amant,
Que c'en était vraiment charmant!

Dansons la gigue!

Mais je trouve encor meilleur
Le baiser de sa bouche en fleur,
Depuis qu'elle est morte à mon coeur.

Dansons la gigue!

Je me souviens, je me souviens
Des heures et des entretiens,
Et c'est le meilleur de mes biens.

Dansons la gigue!

STREETS

Dance the jig!

I loved best her pretty eyes
Clearer than stars in any skies,
I loved her eyes for their dear lies.

Dance the jig!

And ah! the ways, the ways she had
Of driving a poor lover mad:
It made a man's heart sad and glad.

Dance the jig!

But now I find the old kisses shed
From her flower-mouth a rarer red
Now that her heart to mine is dead.

Dance the jig!

And I recall, now I recall
Old days and hours, and ever shall,
And that is best, and best of all.

Dance the jig!

From Jadis et Naguère

ART POÉTIQUE

A Charles Morice.

De la musique avant toute chose,
Et pour cela préfère l'Impair
Plus vague et plus soluble dans l'air,
Sans rien en lui qui pèse ou qui pose.

Il faut aussi que tu n'ailles point
Choisir tes mots sans quelque méprise:
Rien de plus cher que la chanson grise
Où l'Indécis au Précis se joint.

C'est des beaux yeux derrière les voiles,
C'est le grand jour tremblant de midi,
C'est, par un ciel d'automne attiédi,
Le bleu fouillis des claires étoiles!

Car nous voulons la Nuance encor,
Pas la Couleur, rien que la nuance!
Oh! la nuance seule fiance
Le rêve au rêve et la flûte au cor!

Fuis du plus loin la Pointe assassine,
L'Esprit cruel et le rire impur,
Qui font pleurer les yeux de l'Azur,
Et tout cet ail de basse cuisine!

Prends l'éloquence et tords-lui son cou!
Tu feras bien, en train d'énergie,

De rendre un peu la Rime assagie.
Si l'on n'y veille, elle ira jusqu'où?

O qui dira les torts de la Rime!
Quel enfant sourd ou quel nègre fou
Nous a forgé ce bijou d'un sou
Qui sonne creux et faux sous la lime?

De la musique encore et toujours!
Que ton vers soit la chose envolée
Qu'on sent qui fuit d'une âme en allée
Vers d'autres cieux à d'autres amours.

Que ton vers soit la bonne aventure
Éparse au vent crispé du matin
Qui va fleurant la menthe et le thym…
Et tout le reste est littérature.

ART POÉTIQUE

Music first and foremost of all!
Choose your measure of odd not even,
Let it melt in the air of heaven,
Pose not, poise not, but rise and fall.

Choose your words, but think not whether
Each to other of old belong:
What so dear as the dim grey song
Where clear and vague are joined together?

'Tis veils of beauty for beautiful eyes,
'Tis the trembling light of the naked noon,
'Tis a medley of blue and gold, the moon
And stars in the cool of autumn skies.

Let every shape of its shade be born;
Colour, away! come to me, shade!
Only of shade can the marriage be made
Of dream with dream and of flute with horn.

Shun the Point, lest death with it come,
Unholy laughter and cruel wit
(For the eyes of the angels weep at it)
And all the garbage of scullery-scum.

Take Eloquence, and wring the neck of him!
You had better, by force, from time to time,
Put a little sense in the head of Rhyme:
If you watch him not, you will be at the beck of him.

O, who shall tell us the wrongs of Rhyme?
What witless savage or what deaf boy

Has made for us this twopenny toy
Whose bells ring hollow and out of time?

Music always and music still!
Let your verse be the wandering thing
That flutters in flight from a soul on the wing
Towards other skies at a new whim's will.

Let your verse be the luck of the lure
Afloat on the winds that at morning hint
Of the odours of thyme and the savour of mint …
And all the rest is literature.

MEZZETIN, CHANTANT

Va! sans nul autre souci
Que de conserver ta joie!
Fripe les jupes de soie
Et goûte les vers aussi.

La morale la meilleure,
En ce monde où les plus fous
Sont les plus sages de tous,
C'est encor d'oublier l'heure.

Il s'agit de n'être point
Mélancolique et morose.
La vie est-elle une chose
Grave et ruelle à ce point?

MEZZETIN CHANTANT

Go, and with never a care
But the care to keep happiness!
Crumple a silken dress
And snatch a song in the air.

Hear the moral of all the wise
In a world where happy folly
Is wiser than melancholy:
Forget the hour as it flies!

The one thing needful on earth, it
Is not to be whimpering.
Is life after all a thing
Real enough to be worth it?

From Sagesse

I

Les chères mains qui furent miennes,
Toutes petites, toutes belles,
Après ces méprises mortelles
Et toutes ces choses païennes,

Après les rades et les grèves,
Et les pays et les provinces,
Royales mieux qu'au temps des princes,
Les chères mains m'ouvrent les rêves.

Mains en songe, mains sur mon âme,
Sais-je, moi, ce que vous daignâtes,
Parmi ces rumeurs scélérates,
Dire à cette âme qui se pâme?

Ment-elle, ma vision chaste
D'affinité spirituelle,
De complicité maternelle,
D'affection étroite et vaste?

Remords si cher, peine très bonne,
Rêves bénits, mains consacrées,
O ces mains, ces mains vénérées.
Faites le geste qui pardonne!

I

The little hands that once were mine,
The hands I loved, the lovely hands,
After the roadways and the strands,
And realms and kingdoms once divine,

And mortal loss of all that seems
Lost with the old sad pagan things,
Royal as in the days of kings
The dear hands open to me dreams.

Hands of dream, hands of holy flame
Upon my soul in blessing laid,
What is it that these hands have said
That my soul hears and swoons to them?

Is it a phantom, this pure sight
Of mother's love made tenderer,
Of spirit with spirit linked to share
The mutual kinship of delight?

Good sorrow, dear remorse, and ye,
Blest dreams, O hands ordained of heaven
To tell me if I am forgiven,
Make but the sign that pardons me!

II

O mon Dieu, vous m'avez blessé d'amour
Et la blessure est encore vibrante,
O mon Dieu, vous m'avez blessé d'amour!

O mon Dieu, votre crainte m'a frappé
Et la brûlure est encor là qui tonne,
O mon Dieu, votre crainte m'a frappé!

O mon Dieu, j'ai connu que tout est vil
Et votre gloire en moi s'est installée,
O mon Dieu, j'ai connu que tout est vil!

Noyez mon âme aux flots de votre Vin,
Fondez ma vie au Pain de votre table,
Noyez mon âme aux flots de votre Vin.

Voici mon sang que je n'ai pas versé,
Voici ma chair indigne de souffrance,
Voici mon sang que je n'ai pas versé.

Voici mon front qui n'a pu que rougir
Pour l'escabeau de vos pieds adorables,
Voici mon front qui n'a pu que rougir.

Voici mes mains qui n'ont pas travaillé
Pour les charbons ardents et l'encens rare,
Voici mes mains qui n'ont pas travaillé.

Voici mon coeur qui n'a battu qu'en vain,
Pour palpiter aux ronces du Calvaire,
Voici mon coeur qui n'a battu qu'en vain.

Voici mes pieds, frivoles voyageurs,
Pour accourir au cri de votre grâce,
Voici mes pieds, frivoles voyageurs.

Voici ma voix, bruit maussade et menteur,
Pour les reproches de la Pénitence,
Voici ma voix, bruit maussade et menteur.

Voici mes yeux, luminaires d'erreur,
Pour être éteints aux pleurs de la prière,
Voici mes yeux, luminaires d'erreur.

Hélas, Vous, Dieu d'offrande et de pardon,
Quel est le puits de mon ingratitude,
Hélas! Vous, Dieu d'offrande et de pardon!

Dieu de terreur et Dieu de sainteté,
Hélas! ce noir abîme de mon crime,
Dieu de terreur et Dieu de sainteté,

Vous, Dieu de paix, de joie et de bonheur,
Toutes mes peurs, toutes mes ignorances,
Vous, Dieu de paix, de joie et de bonheur,

Vous connaissez tout cela, tout cela,
Et que je suis plus pauvre que personne,
Vous connaissez tout cela, tout cela,

Mais ce que j'ai, mon Dieu, je vous le donne.

II

O my God, thou hast wounded me with love,
Behold the wound, that is still vibrating,
O my God, thou hast wounded me with love.

O my God, thy fear hath fallen upon me,
Behold the burn is there, and it throbs aloud,
O my God, thy fear hath fallen upon me.

O my God, I have known that all is vile
And that thy glory hath stationed itself in me,
O my God, I have known that all is vile.

Drown my soul in floods, floods of thy wine,
Mingle my life with the body of thy bread,
Drown my soul in floods, floods of thy wine.

Take my blood, that I have not poured out,
Take my flesh, unworthy of suffering,
Take my blood, that I have not poured out.

Take my brow, that has only learned to blush,
To be the footstool of thine adorable feet,
Take my brow, that has only learned to blush.

Take my hands, because they have laboured not
For coals of fire and for rare frankincense,
Take my hands, because they have laboured not.

Take my heart, that has beaten for vain things,
To throb under the thorns of Calvary,
Take my heart that has beaten for vain things.

Take my feet, frivolous travellers,
That they may run to the crying of thy grace,
Take my feet, frivolous travellers.

Take my voice, a harsh and a lying noise,
For the reproaches of thy Penitence,
Take my voice, a harsh and a lying noise

Take mine eyes, luminaries of deceit,
That they may be extinguished in the tears of prayer,
Take mine eyes, luminaries of deceit.

Alas, thou, God of pardon and promises,
What is the pit of mine ingratitude,
Alas, thou, God of pardon and promises.

God of terror and God of holiness,
Alas, my sinfulness is a black abyss,
God of terror and God of holiness.

Thou, God of peace, of joy and delight,
All my tears, all my ignorances,
Thou, God of peace, of joy and delight.

Thou, O God, knowest all this, all this,
How poor I am, poorer than any man,
Thou, O God, knowest all this, all this.

And what I have, my God, I give to thee.

III

Un grand sommeil noir
Tombe sur ma vie:
Dormez, tout espoir,
Dormez, toute envie!

Je ne vois plus rien,
Je perds la mémoire
Du mal et du bien…
O la triste histoire!

Je suis un berceau
Qu'une main balance
Au creux d'un caveau:
Silence, silence!

III

Slumber dark and deep
Falls across my life;
I will put to sleep
Hope, desire, and strife.

All things pass away,
Good and evil seem
To my soul to-day
Nothing but a dream;

I a cradle laid
In a hollow cave,
By a great hand swayed:
Silence, like the grave.

IV

La tristesse, langueur du corps humain
M'attendrissent, me fléchissent, m'apitoient,
Ah! surtout quand des sommeils noirs le foudroient.
Quand les draps zèbrent la peau, foulent la main!
Et que mièvre dans la fièvre du demain,
Tiède encor du bain de sueur qui décroît,
Comme un oiseau qui grelotte sous un toit!
Et les pieds, toujours douloureux du chemin,

Et le sein, marqué d'un double coup de poing,
Et la bouche, une blessure rouge encor,
Et la chair frémissante, frêle décor,
Et les yeux, les pauvres yeux si beaux où point
La douleur de voir encore du fini!…
Triste corps! Combien faible et combien puni!

IV

The body's sadness and the languor thereof
Melt and bow me with pity till I could weep,
Ah! when the dark hours break it down in sleep
And the bedclothes score the skin and the hot hands move;
Alert for a little with the fever of day,
Damp still with the heavy sweat of the night that has thinned,
Like a bird that trembles on a roof in the wind:
And the feet that are sorrowful because of the way,

And the breast that a hand has scarred with a double blow,
And the mouth that as an open wound is red,
And the flesh that shivers and is a painted show,
And the eyes, poor eyes so lovely with tears unshed
For the sorrow of seeing this also over and done:
Sad body, how weak and how punished under the sun!

V

La mer est plus belle
Que les cathédrales,
Nourrice fidèle,
Berceuse de râles,
La mer qui prie
La Vierge Marie!

Elle a tous les dons
Terribles et doux.
J'entends ses pardons
Gronder ses courroux.
Cette immensité
N'a rien d'entêté.

O! si patiente,
Même quand méchante!
Un souffle ami hante
La vague, et nous chante:
«Vous sans espérance,
Mourez sans souffrance!»

Et puis sous les cieux
Qui s'y rient plus clairs,
Elle a des airs bleus,
Rosés, gris et verts…
Plus belle que tous,
Meilleure que nous!

V

Fairer is the sea
Than the minster high,
Faithful nurse is she,
And last lullaby,
And the Virgin prays
Over the sea's ways.

Gifts of grief and guerdons
From her bounty come,
And I hear her pardons
Chide her angers home;
Nothing in her is
Unforgivingness.

She is piteous,
She the perilous!
Friendly things to us
The wave sings to us:
You whose hope is past,
Here is peace at last.

And beneath the skies,
Brighter-hued than they,
She has azure dyes,
Rose and green and grey.
Better is the sea
Than all fair things or we.

IMPRESSION FAUSSE

Dame souris trotte,
Noire dans le gris du soir,
Dame souris trotte
Grise dans le noir.

On sonne la cloche,
Dormez, les bons prisonniers!
On sonne la cloche:
Faut que vous dormiez.

Pas de mauvais rêve,
Ne pensez qu'à vos amours
Pas de mauvais rêve:
Les belles toujours!

Le grand clair de lune!
On ronfle ferme à côté.
Le grand clair de lune
En réalité!

Un nuage passe,
Il fait noir comme en un four.
Un nuage passe.
Tiens, le petit jour!

Dame souris trotte,
Rose dans les rayons bleus.
Dame souris trotte:
Debout, paresseux!

From Parallèlement:

IMPRESSION FAUSSE

Little lady mouse,
Black upon the grey of light;
Little lady mouse,
Grey upon the night.

Now they ring the bell,
All good prisoners slumber deep;
Now they ring the bell,
Nothing now but sleep.

Only pleasant dreams,
Love's enough for thinking of;
Only pleasant dreams,
Long live love!

Moonlight over all,
Someone snoring heavily;
Moonlight over all
In reality.

Now there comes a cloud,
It is dark as midnight here;
Now there comes a cloud,
Dawn begins to peer.

Little lady mouse,
Rosy in a ray of blue,
Little lady mouse:
Up now, all of you!

"TU CROIS AU MARC DE CAFÉ"

Tu crois au marc de café,
Aux présages, aux grands jeux:
Moi je ne crois qu'en tes grand yeux.

Tu crois aux contes de fées,
Aux jours néfastes, aux songes,
Moi je ne crois qu'en tes mensonges.

Tu crois en un vague Dieu,
En quelque saint spécial,
En tel *Ave* contre tel mal.

Je ne crois qu'aux heures bleues
Et roses que tu n'épanches
Dans le volupté des nuits blanches!

Et si profonde est ma foi
Envers tout ce que je croi
Que je ne vis plus que pour toi.

From Chansons Pour Elle

"YOU BELIEVE THAT THERE MAY BE LUCK"

You believe that there may be
Luck in strangers in the tea:
I believe only in your eyes.

You believe in fairy-tales,
Days one wins and days one fails:
I believe only in your lies.

You believe in heavenly powers,
In some saint to whom one prays
Or in some Ave that one says.

I believe only in the hours,
Coloured with the rosy lights
You rain for me on sleepless nights.

And so firmly I receive
These for truth, that I believe
That only for your sake I live.

"QUAND NOUS IRONS"

Quand nous irons, si je dois encor la voir,
Dans l'obscurité du bois noir,

Quand nous serons ivres d'air et de lumière
Au bord de la claire rivière,

Quand nous serons d'un moment dépaysés
De ce Paris aux cœurs brisés,

Et si la bonté lente de la nature
Nous berce d'un rêve qui dure,

Alors, allons dormir du dernier sommeill
Dieu se chargera du réveil.

From Epigrammes

"WHEN WE GO TOGETHER"

When we go together, if I may see her again,
Into the dark wood and the rain;

When we are drunken with air and the sun's delight
At the brink of the river of light;

When we are homeless at last, for a moment's space
Without city or abiding-place;

And if the slow good-will of the world still seem
To cradle us in a dream;

Then, let us sleep the last sleep with no leave-taking,
And God will see to the waking.

Henri Fantin-Latour, The Corner of the Table, 1872,
Musée d'Orsay, Paris

PAUL VERLAINE

By Arthur Symons

(From *The Symbolist Movement In Literature*)

1

"*Bien affectueusement* ... yours, P. Verlaine." So, in its gay and friendly mingling of French and English, ended the last letter I had from Verlaine. A few days afterwards came the telegram from Paris telling me of his death, in the Rue Descartes, on that 8th January, 1896.

"Condemned to death," as he was, in Victor Hugo's phrase of men in general, "with a sort of indefinite reprieve," and gravely ill as I had for some time known him to be, it was still with a shock, not only of sorrow, but of surprise, that I heard the news of his death. He had suffered and survived so much, and I found it so hard to associate the idea of death with one who had always been so passionately in love with life, more passionately in love with life than any man I ever knew. Rest was one of the delicate privileges of life which he never loved: he did but endure it with grumbling gaiety when a hospital-bed claimed him. And whenever he spoke to me of the long rest which has now sealed his eyelids, it was with a shuddering revolt from the thought of ever going away into the cold, out of the sunshine which had been so warm to him. With all his pains, misfortunes, and the calamities which followed him step by step all his life, I think few men ever got so much out of their lives, or lived so fully, so intensely, with such a genius for living. That, indeed, is why he was a great poet. Verlaine was a man who gave its full value to every moment, who got out of every moment all that that moment had to give him. It was not always, not often, perhaps, pleasure. But it was energy, the vital force of a nature which was always receiving and giving out, never at rest, never passive, or indifferent, or hesitating. It is impossible for me to convey to those who did not know him any notion of how sincere he was. The word "sincerity" seems hardly to have emphasis enough to say, in regard to this one man, what it says, adequately enough, of others. He sinned, and it was with all his humanity; he repented, and it was with all his soul. And to every occurrence of the day, to every mood of the mind, to every impulse of the creative instinct, he brought the same unparalleled sharpness of sensation. When, in 1894, he was my guest in London, I was amazed by the exactitude of his memory of the mere turnings of the streets, the shapes and colours of the buildings, which he had not seen for twenty years. He saw, he felt, he remembered, everything, with an unconscious mental selection of the fine shades, the essential part of things, or precisely those aspects which most other people would pass by.

Few poets of our time have been more often drawn, few have been easier to draw, few have better repaid drawing, than Paul Verlaine. A face without a beautiful line, a face all character, full of somnolence and sudden fire, in which every irregularity was a kind of aid to the hand, could not but tempt the artist desiring at once to render a significant likeness and to have his own part in the creation of a picture. Verlaine, like all men of genius, had something of the air of the somnambulist: that profound slumber of the face, as it was in him, with its startling awakenings. It was a face devoured by dreams, feverish and somnolent; it had earthly passion, intellectual pride, spiritual humility; the air of one who remembers, not without an effort, who is listening, half distractedly to something which other people do not hear; coming back so suddenly, and from so far, with the relief of one who steps out of that obscure shadow into the noisier forgetfulness of life. The eyes, often half closed, were like the eyes of a cat between sleeping and waking; eyes in which contemplation was "itself an act." A remarkable lithograph by Mr. Rothenstein (the face lit by oblique eyes, the folded hands thrust into the cheek) gives with singular truth the sensation of that restless watch on things which this prisoner of so many chains kept without slackening. To Verlaine every corner of the world was alive with tempting and consoling and terrifying beauty. I have never known any one to whom the sight of the eyes was so intense and imaginative a thing. To him, physical sight and spiritual vision, by some strange alchemical operation of the brain, were one. And in the disquietude of his face, which seemed to take such close heed of things, precisely because it was sufficiently apart from them to be always a spectator, there was a realisable process of vision continually going on, in which all the loose ends of the visible world were being caught up into a new mental fabric.

And along with this fierce subjectivity, into which the egoism of the artist entered so unconsciously, and in which it counted for so much, there was more than the usual amount of childishness, always in some measure present in men of genius. There was a real, almost blithe, childishness in the way in which he would put on his "Satanic" expression, of which it was part of the joke that every one should not be quite in the secret. It was a whim of this kind which made him put at the beginning of *Romances sans Paroles* that very criminal image of a head which had so little resemblance with even the shape, indeed curious enough, of his actual head. "Born under the sign of Saturn," as he no doubt was, with that "old prisoner's head" of which he tells us, it was by his amazing faculty for a simple kind of happiness that he always impressed me. I have never seen so cheerful an invalid as he used to be at that hospital, the Hôpital Saint-Louis, where at one time I used to go and see him every week. His whole face seemed to chuckle as he would tell me, in his emphatic, confiding way, everything that entered into his head; the droll stories cut short by a groan, a lamentation, a sudden fury of reminiscence, at which his face would cloud or convulse, the wild eyebrows slanting up and down; and then, suddenly, the good laugh would be back, clearing the air. No one was ever so responsive to his own moods as Verlaine, and with him every mood had the vehemence of a passion. Is not his whole art a delicate waiting upon moods, with that perfect confidence in them as they are, which it is a large part of ordinary education to discourage in us, and a large part of experience to repress? But to Verlaine, happily, experience taught nothing; or rather, it taught him only to cling the more closely to those moods in whose succession lies the more intimate part of our spiritual life. It is no doubt well for society that man should learn by experience; for the artist the benefit is doubtful. The artist, it cannot be too clearly understood, has no more part in society than a monk in domestic life: he cannot be judged by its rules, he can be neither praised not blamed for his acceptance or rejection of its conventions. Social rules are made by normal people for normal people, and the man of genius is fundamentally abnormal. It is the poet against society, society against the poet, a direct antagonism; the shock of which, however, it is often possible to avoid by a compromise. So much licence is allowed on the one side, so much liberty foregone on the other. The consequences are not always of the best, art being generally the loser. But there are certain natures to which compromise is impossible; and the nature of Verlaine was one of these natures.

"The soul of an immortal child," says one who has understood him better than others, Charles Morice, "that is the soul of Verlaine, with all the privileges and all the perils of so being; with the sudden despair so easily distracted, the vivid gaieties without a cause, the excessive suspicions and the excessive confidences, the whims so easily outwearied, the deaf and blind infatuations, with, especially, the unceasing renewal of impressions in the incorruptible integrity of personal vision and sensation. Years, influences, teachings, may pass over a temperament such as this, may irritate it, may fatigue it; transform it, never – never so much as to alter that particular unity which consists in a dualism, in the division of forces between the longing after what is evil and the adoration of what is good; or rather, in the antagonism of spirit and flesh. Other men 'arrange' their lives, take sides, follow one direction; Verlaine hesitates before a choice, which seems to him monstrous, for, with the integral *naïveté* of irrefutable human truth, he cannot resign himself, however strong may be the doctrine, however enticing may be the passion, to the necessity of sacrificing one to the other, and from one to the other he oscillates without a moment's repose."

It is in such a sense as this that Verlaine may be said to have learnt nothing from experience, in the sense that he learnt everything direct from life, and without comparing day with day. That the exquisite artist of the *Fêtes Galantes* should become the great poet of *Sagesse,* it was needful that things should have happened as disastrously as they did: the marriage with the girl-wife, that brief idyl, the passion for drink, those other forbidden passions, vagabondage, an attempted crime, the eighteen months of prison, conversion; followed, as it had to be, by relapse, bodily sickness, poverty, beggary almost, a lower and lower descent into mean distresses. It was needful that all this should happen, in order that the spiritual vision should eclipse the material vision; but it was needful that all this should happen in vain, so far as the conduct of life was concerned. Reflection, in Verlaine, is pure waste; it is the speech of the soul and the speech of the eyes, that we must listen to in his verse, never the speech of the reason. And I call him fortunate because, going through life with a great unconsciousness of what most men spend their lives in considering, he was able to abandon himself entirely to himself, to his unimpeded vision, to his unchecked emotion, to the passionate sincerity which in him was genius.

2

French poetry, before Verlaine, was an admirable vehicle for a really fine, a really poetical, kind of rhetoric. With Victor Hugo, for the first time since Ronsard (the two or three masterpieces of Ronsard and his companions) it had learnt to sing; with Baudelaire it had invented a new vocabulary for the expression of subtle, often perverse, essentially modern emotion and sensation. But with Victor Hugo, with Baudelaire, we are still under the dominion of rhetoric. "Take eloquence, and wring its neck!" said Verlaine in his *Art Poétique;* and he showed, by writing it, that French verse could be written without rhetoric. It was partly from his study of English models that he learnt the secret of liberty in verse, but it was much more a secret found by the way, in the mere endeavour to be absolutely sincere, to express exactly what he saw, to give voice to his own temperament, in which intensity of feeling seemed to find its own expression, as if by accident. *L'art, mes enfants, c'est d'être absolument soi-même,* he tells us in one of his later poems; and, with such a personality as Verlaine's to express, what more has art to do, if it would truly, and in any interesting manner, hold the mirror up to nature?

For, consider the natural qualities which this man had for the task of creating a new poetry. "Sincerity, and the impression of the moment followed to the letter": that is how he defined his theory of style, in an article written about himself.

> Car nous voulons la nuance encor,
> Pas la couleur, rien que la nuance!

as he cries, in his famous *Art Poétique*. Take, then, his susceptibility of the senses, an emotional susceptibility not less delicate; a life sufficiently troubled to draw out every emotion of which he was capable, and, with it, that absorption in the moment, that inability to look before or after; the need to love and the need to confess, each a passion; an art of painting the fine shades of landscape, of evoking atmosphere, which can be compared only with the art of Whistler; a simplicity of language which is the direct outcome of a simplicity of temperament, with just enough consciousness of itself for a final elegance; and, at the very depth of his being, an almost fierce humility, by which the passion of love, after searching furiously through all his creatures, finds God by the way, and kneels in the dust before him. Verlaine was never a theorist: he left theories to Mallarmé. He had only his divination; and he divined that poetry, always desiring that miracles should happen, had never waited patiently enough upon the miracle. It was by that proud and humble mysticism of his temperament that he came to realise how much could be done by, In a sense, trying to do nothing.

And then: *De la musique avant toute chose; De la musique encore et toujours!* There are poems of Verlaine which go as far as verse can go to become pure music, the voice of a bird with a human soul. It is part of his simplicity, his divine childishness, that he abandons himself, at times, to the song which words begin to sing in the air, with the same wise confidence with which he abandons himself to the other miracles about him. He knows that words are living things, which we have not created, and which go their way without demanding of us the right to live. He knows that words are suspicious, not without their malice, and that they resist mere force with the impalpable resistance of fire or water. They are to be caught only with guile or with trust. Verlaine has both, and words become Ariel to him. They bring him not only that submission of the slave which they bring to others, but all the soul, and in a happy bondage. They transform themselves for him into music, colour, and shadow; a disembodied music, diaphanous colours, luminous shadow. They serve him with so absolute a self-negation that he can write *romances sans paroles,* songs almost without words, in which scarcely a sense of the interference of human speech remains. The ideal of lyric poetry, certainly, is to be this passive, flawless medium for the deeper consciousness of things, the mysterious voice of that mystery which lies about us, out of which we have come, and into which we shall return. It is not without reason that we cannot analyse a perfect lyric.

With Verlaine the sense of hearing and the sense of sight are almost interchangeable: he paints with sound, and his line and atmosphere become music. It was with the most precise accuracy that Whistler applied the terms of music to his painting, for painting, when it aims at being the vision of reality, *pas la couleur, rien que la nuance,* passes almost into the condition of music. Verlaine's landscape painting is always an evocation, in which outline is lost in atmosphere.

> C'est des beaux yeux derrière des voiles,
> C'est le grand jour tremblant de midi,
> C'est, par un ciel d'automne attiédi,
> Le bleu fouillis des claires étoiles!

He was a man, certainly, "for whom the visible world existed," but for whom it existed always as a vision. He absorbed it through all his senses, as the true mystic absorbs the divine beauty. And so he created in verse a new voice for nature, full of the humble ecstasy with which he saw, listened, accepted.

> Cette âme qui se lamente
> En cette plaine dormante
>   C'est la nôtre, n'est-ce pas?
> La mienne, dis, et la tienne,
> Dont s'exhale l'humble antienne
>   Par ce tiède soir, tout bas?

And with the same attentive simplicity with which he found words for the sensations of hearing and the sensations of sight, he found words for the sensations of the soul, for the fine shades of feeling. From the moment when his inner life may be said to have begun, he was occupied with the task of an unceasing confession, in which one seems to overhear him talking to himself, in that vague, preoccupied way which he often had. Here again are words which startle one by their delicate resemblance to thoughts, by their winged flight from so far, by their alighting so close. The verse murmurs, with such an ingenuous confidence, such intimate secrets. That "setting free" of verse, which is one of the achievements of Verlaine, was itself mainly an attempt to be more and more sincere, a way of turning poetic artifice to new account, by getting back to nature itself, hidden away under the eloquent rhetoric of Hugo, Baudelaire, and the Parnassians. In the devotion of rhetoric to either beauty or truth, there is a certain consciousness of an audience, of an external judgment: rhetoric would convince, be admired. It is the very essence of poetry to be unconscious of anything between its own moment of flight and the supreme beauty which it will never attain. Verlaine taught French poetry that wise and subtle unconsciousness. It was in so doing that he "fused his personality," in the words of Verhaeren, "so profoundly with beauty, that he left upon it the imprint of a new and henceforth eternal attitude."

3

J'ai la fureur d'aimer, says Verlaine, in a passage of very personal significance.

> J'ai la fureur d'aimer. Mon cœur si faible est fou.
> N'importe quand, n'importe quel et n'importe où,
> Qu'un éclair de beauté, de vertu, de vaillance,
> Luise, il s'y précipite, il y vole, il y lance,
> Et, le temps d'une étreinte, il embrasse cent fois
> L'être ou l'objet qu'il a poursuivi de son choix;
> Puis, quand l'illusion a replié son aile,
> Il revient triste et seul bien souvent, mais fidèle,
> Et laissant aux ingrats quelque chose de lui,
> Sang ou chair….
> J'ai la fureur d'aimer. Qu'y faire? Ah, laissez faire!

And certainly this admirable, and supremely dangerous, quality was at the root of Verlaine's nature. Instinctive, unreasoning as he was, entirely at the mercy of the emotion or impression which, for the moment, had seized upon him, it was inevitable that he should be completely at the mercy of the most imperious of instincts, of passions, and of intoxications. And he had the simple and ardent nature, in this again consistently childlike, to which love, some kind of affection, given or returned, is not the luxury, the exception, which it is to many natures, but a daily necessity. To such a temperament there may or may not be the one great passion; there will certainly be many passions. And in Verlaine I find that single, childlike necessity of loving and being loved, all through his life and on every page of his works; I find it, unchanged in essence, but constantly changing form, in his chaste and unchaste devotions to women, in his passionate friendships with men, in his supreme mystical adoration of God.

To turn from *La Bonne Chanson,* written for a wedding present to a young wife, to *Chansons pour Elle,* written more than twenty years later, in dubious honour of a middle-aged mistress, is to travel a long road, the hard, long road which Verlaine had travelled during those years. His life was ruinous, a disaster, more sordid perhaps than the life of any other poet; and he could write of it, from a hospital-bed, with this quite sufficient sense of its deprivations. "But all the same, it is hard," he laments, in *Mes Hôpitaux,* "after a life of work, set off, I admit, with accidents in which I have had a large share, catastrophes perhaps vaguely premeditated – it is hard, I say, at forty-seven years of age, in full possession of all the reputation (of the *success,* to use the frightful current phrase) to which my highest ambitions could aspire – hard, hard, hard indeed, worse than hard, to find myself – good God! – to find myself *on the streets,* and to have nowhere to lay my head and support an ageing body save the pillows and the *menus* of a public charity, even now uncertain, and which might at any moment be withdrawn – God forbid! – without, apparently, the fault of any one, oh! not even, and above all, not mine." Yet, after all, these sordid miseries, this poor man's vagabondage, all the misfortunes of one certainly "irreclaimable," on which so much stress has been laid, alike by friends and by foes, are externalities; they are not the man; the man, the eternal lover, passionate and humble, remains unchanged, while only his shadow wanders, from morning to night of the long day.

The poems to Rimbaud, to Lucien Létinois, to others, the whole volume of *Dédicaces,* cover perhaps as wide a range of sentiment as *La Bonne Chanson* and *Chansons pour Elle.* The poetry of friendship has never been sung with such plaintive sincerity, such simple human feeling, as in some of these poems, which can only be compared, in modern poetry, with a poem for which Verlaine had a great admiration, Tennyson's *In Memoriam.* Only with Verlaine, the thing itself, the affection or the regret, is everything; there is no room for meditation over destiny, or search for a problematical consolation. Other poems speak a more difficult language, in which, doubtless, *l'ennui de vivre avec les gens et dans les choses* counts for much, and *la fureur d'aimer* for more.

In spite of the general impression to the contrary, an

impression which by no means displeased him himself, I must contend that the sensuality of Verlaine, brutal as it could sometimes be, was after all simple rather than complicated, instinctive rather than perverse, in the poetry of Baudelaire, with which the poetry of Verlaine is so often compared, there is a deliberate science of sensual perversity which has something almost monachal in its accentuation of vice with horror, in its passionate devotion to passions. Baudelaire brings every complication of taste, the exasperation of; perfumes, the irritant of cruelty, the very odours and colours of corruption, to the creation and adornment of a sort of religion, in which an eternal mass is served before a veiled altar. There is no confession, no absolution, not a prayer is permitted which is not set down in the ritual. With Verlaine, however often love may pass into sensuality, to whatever length sensuality may be hurried, sensuality is never more than the malady of love. It is love desiring the absolute, seeking in vain, seeking always, and, finally, out of the depths, finding God.

Verlaine's conversion took place while he was in prison, during those solitary eighteen months in company with his thoughts, that enforced physical inactivity, which could but concentrate his whole energy on the only kind of sensation then within his capacity, the sensations of the soul and of the conscience. With that promptitude of abandonment which was his genius, he grasped feverishly at the succour of God and the Church, he abased himself before the immaculate purity of the Virgin. He had not, like others who have risen from the same depths to the same height of humiliation, to despoil his nature of its pride, to conquer his intellect, before he could become *l'enfant vêtu de laine et d'innocence*. All that was simple, humble, childlike in him accepted that humiliation with the loving child's joy in penitence; all that was ardent, impulsive, indomitable in him burst at once into a flame of adoration.

He realised the great secret of the Christian mystics: that it is possible to love God with an extravagance of the whole being, to which the love of the creature cannot attain. All love is an attempt to break through the loneliness of individuality, to fuse oneself with something not oneself, to give and to receive, in all the warmth of natural desire, that inmost element which remains, so cold and so invincible, in the midst of the soul. It is a desire of the infinite in humanity, and, as humanity has its limits, it can but return sadly upon itself when that limit is reached. Thus human love is not only an ecstasy but a despair, and the more profound a despair the more ardently it is returned.

But the love of God, considered only from its human aspect, contains at least the illusion of infinity. To love God is to love the absolute, so far as the mind of man can conceive the absolute, and thus, in a sense, to love God is to possess the absolute, for love has already possessed that which it apprehends. What the earthly lover realises to himself as the image of his beloved is, after all, his own vision of love, not her. God must remain *deus absconditus,* even to love; but the lover, incapable of possessing infinity, will have possessed all of infinity of which he is capable. And his ecstasy will be flawless. The human mind, meditating on infinity, can but discover perfection beyond perfection; for it is impossible to conceive of limitation in any aspect of that which has once been conceived as infinite. In place of that deception which comes from the shock of a boundary-line beyond which humanity cannot conceive of humanity, there is only a divine rage against the limits of human perception, which by their own failure seem at last to limit for us the infinite itself. For once, love finds itself bounded only by its own capacity; so far does the love of God exceed the love of the creature, and so far would it exceed that love if God did not exist.

But if He does exist! if, outside humanity, a conscient, eternal perfection, who has made the world in his image, loves the humanity He has made, and demands love in return! If the spirit of his love is as a breath over the world, suggesting, strengthening, the love which it desires, seeking man that man may seek God, itself the impulse which it humbles itself to accept at man's hands; if indeed,

> Mon Dieu m'a dit: mon fils, il faut m'aimer;

how much more is this love of God, in its inconceivable acceptance and exchange, the most divine, the only unending intoxication, in the world! Well, it is this realised sense of communion, point by point realised, and put into words, more simple, more human, more instinctive than any poet since the mediæval mystics has found for the delights of this intercourse, that we find in *Sagesse,* and in the other religious poems of Verlaine.

But, with Verlaine, the love of God is not merely a rapture, it is a thanksgiving for forgiveness. Lying in wait behind all the fair appearances of the world, he remembers the old enemy, the flesh; and the sense of sin (that strange paradox of the reason) is childishly strong in him. He laments his offence, he sees not only the love but the justice of God, and it seems to him, as in a picture, that the little hands of the Virgin are clasped in petition for him. Verlaine's religion is the religion of the Middle Ages. *Je suis catholique,* he said to me, *mais ... catholique du moyen-âge!* He might have written the ballad which Villon made for his mother, and with the same visual sense of heaven and hell. Like a child, he tells his sins over, promises that he has put them behind him, and finds such *naïve,* human words to express his gratitude. The Virgin is really, to him, mother and friend; he delights in the simple, peasant humanity, still visible in her who is also the Mystical Rose, the Tower of Ivory, the Gate of Heaven, and who now extends her hands, in the gesture of pardon, from a throne only just lower than the throne of God.

4

Experience, I have said, taught Verlaine nothing; religion had no more stable influence upon his conduct then experience. In that apology for himself which he wrote under the anagram of "Pauvre Lelian," he has stated the case with his usual sincerity. "I believe," he says, "and I sin in thought as in action; I believe, and I repent in thought, if no more. Or again, I believe, and I am a good Christian at this moment; I believe, and I am a bad Christian the instant after. The remembrance, the hope, the invocation of a sin delights me, with or without remorse, sometimes under the very form of sin, and hedged with all its natural consequences; more often – so strong, so natural and *animal,* are flesh and blood – just in the same manner as the remembrances, hopes, invocations of any carnal freethinker. This delight, I, you, some one else, writers, it pleases us to put to paper and publish more or less well expressed: we consign it, in short, into literary form, forgetting all religious ideas, or not letting one of them escape us. Can any one in good faith condemn us as poet? A hundred times no." And, indeed, I would echo, a hundred times no! It is just this apparent complication of what is really a great simplicity which gives its singular value to the poetry of Verlaine, permitting it to sum up in itself the whole paradox of humanity, and especially the weak, passionate, uncertain, troubled century to which we belong, in which so many doubts, negations, and distresses seem, now more than ever, to be struggling towards at least an ideal of spiritual consolation. Verlaine is the poet of these weaknesses and of that ideal.

BIBLIOGRAPHY AND NOTES

PAUL VERLAINE
(1844-1896)

Poèmes Saturniens, 1866; *Fêtes Galantes,* 1869; *La Bonne Chanson,* 1870; *Romances sans Paroles,* 1874; *Sagesse,* 1881; *Les Poètes Maudits,* 1884; *Jadis et Naguère,* 1884; *Les Mémoires d'un Veuf,* 1886; *Louise Leclercq* (**suivi de** *Le Poteau, Pierre Duchatelet, Madame Aubin),* 1887; *Amour,* 1888; *Parallèlement,* 1889; *Dédicaces,* 1890; *Bonheur,* 1891; *Mes Hôpitaux,* 1891; *Chansons pour Elle,* 1891; *Liturgies Intimes,* 1892; *Mes Prisons,* 1893; *Odes en son Honneur,* 1893; *Elégies,* 1893; *Quinze Jours en Hollande,* 1894; *Dans les Limbes,* 1894; *Epigrammes,* 1894; *Confessions,* 1895; *Chair,* 1896; *Invectives,* 1896; *Voyage en France d'un Français* (posthumous), 1907.

The complete works of Verlaine are now published in six volumes at the Librairie Léon Vanier (now Messein); the text is very incorrectly printed, and it is still necessary to refer to the earlier editions in separate volumes. *A Choix de Poésies,*1891, with a preface by François Coppée, and a reproduction of Carrière's admirable portrait, is published in one volume by Charpentier; the series of *Hommes d'Aujourd'hui* contains twenty-seven biographical notices by Verlaine; and a considerable number of poems and prose articles exists, scattered in various magazines, some of them English, such as the *Senate;* in some cases the articles themselves are translated into English, such as "My Visit to London," in the *Savoy* for April, 1896, and "Notes on England: Myself as a French Master," and "Shakespeare and Racine," in the *Fortnightly Review* for July, 1894, and September, 1894. The first English translation in verse from Verlaine is Arthur O'Shaughnessy's rendering of "Clair de Lune" in *Fêtes Galantes*, under the title "Pastel," in *Songs of a Worker*, 1881. A volume of translations in verse, *Poems of Verlaine*, by Gertrude Hall, was published in America in 1895. In Mr. John Gray's *Silverpoints*, 1893, there are translations of "Parsifal," "A Crucifix," "Le Chevalier Malheur," "Spleen," "Clair de Lune," "Mon Dieu m'a dit," and "Green."

As I have mentioned, there have been many portraits of Verlaine. The three portraits drawn on lithographic paper by Mr. Rothenstein, and published in 1898, are but the latest, if also among the best, of a long series, of which Mr. Rothenstein himself has done two or three others, one of which was reproduced in the *Pall Mall Gazette* in 1894, when Verlaine was in London. M. F. A. Cazals, a young artist who was one of Verlaine's most intimate friends, has done I should not like to say how many portraits, some of which he has gathered together in a little book, *Paul Verlaine: ses Portraits*, 1898. There are portraits in nine of Verlaine's own books, several of them by M. Cazals (roughly jotted, expressive notes of moments), one by M. Anquetin (a strong piece of thinking flesh and blood), and in the *Choix de Poésies* there is a reproduction of the cloudy, inspired poet of M. Eugène Carrière's painting. Another portrait, which I have not seen, but which Verlaine himself calls, in the *Dédicaces, un portrait enfin reposé*, was done by M. Aman-Jean. M. Niederhausern has done a bust in bronze, Mr. Rothenstein a portrait medallion. A new edition of the *Confessions*, 1899, contains a number of sketches; *Verlaine Dessinateur*, 1896, many more; and there are yet others in the extremely objectionable book of M. Charles Donos, *Verlaine Intime*, 1898. The *Hommes d'Aujourd'hui* contains a caricature-portrait, many other portraits have appeared in French and English and German and Italian magazines, and there is yet another portrait in the admirable little book of Charles Morice, *Paul Verlaine,* 1888, which contains by far the best study that has ever been made of Verlaine as a poet. I believe Mr. George Moore's article, "A Great Poet," reprinted in *Impressions and Opinions,* 1891, was the first that was written on Verlaine in England; my own article in the *National Review* in 1892 was, I believe, the first detailed study of the whole of his work up to that date. At last, in the *Vie de Paul Verlaine,* of Edmund Lepelletier, there has come the authentic record.

An honest and instructed life of Verlaine has long been wanted, if only as an antidote to the defamatory production called *Verlaine Intime,* made up out of materials collected by the publisher Léon Vanier in his own defense, in order that a hard taskmaster might be presented to the world in the colours of a benefactor. A "legend" which may well have seemed plausible to those who knew Verlaine only at the end of his life, has obtained currency; and a comparison of Verlaine with Villon, not only as a poet (which is to his honour), but also as a man, has been made, and believed. Lepelletier's book is an exact chronicle of a friendship which lasted, without a break, for thirty-six years – that is, from the time when Verlaine was sixteen to the time of his death; and a more sane, loyal and impartial chronicle of any man's life we have never read. It is written with full knowledge of every part of the career which it traces; and it is written by a man who puts down whatever he knows exactly as he believes it to have been. His conclusion is that "on peut fouiller sa vie au microscope: on y reconnaîtra des fautes, des folies, des faiblesses, bien des souffrances aussi, avec de la fatalité au fond, pas de honte véritable, pas une vile et indigne action. Les vrais amis du poète peuvent donc revendiquer pour lui l'épithete d'honnête homme, sans doute très vulgaire, mais qui, aux yeux de certains, a encore du prix."

In 1886 Verlaine dedicated *Les Mémoires d'un Veuf* to Lepelletier, affirming the resolve, on his part, to "garder intacte la vielle amitié si forte et si belle." The compact has been kept nobly by the survivor.

It may, indeed, be questioned whether Lepelletier does not insist a little too much on the bourgeois element which he finds in Verlaine. When a man has suffered under unjust accusations, it is natural for his friends to defend him under whatever aspect seems to them most generally convincing. So it is interesting to know that for seven years Verlaine was in a municipal office, the Bureau des Budgets et Comptes, and that later, in 1882, he made an application, which was refused, for leave to return to his former post. Lepelletier reproaches the authorities for an action which he takes to have precipitated Verlaine into the final misery of his vagabondage. He would have lived quietly, he says, and written in security. Both assumptions may be doubted. What was bourgeois, and contented with quiet, was a small part of the nature of one who was too strong as well as too weak to remain within limits. The terrible force of Verlaine's weakness would always, in the process of making him a poet, have carried him far from that "tranquilité d'une sinécure bureaucratique" which Lepelletier strangely regrets for him. It is hardly permitted, in looking back over a disastrous life which has expressed itself in notable poetry, to regret that the end should have been attained, by no matter what means.

On moral questions Lepelletier speaks with the authority of an intimate friendship, and from a point of view which seems wholly without prejudice. He defends Verlaine with evident conviction against the most serious charges brought against him, and he shows at least, on documentary evidence, that nothing of the darker part of his "legend" was ever proved against him in any of his arrests and imprisonments. Drink, and mad rages let loose by drink, account, ignobly enough, for all of them. In the famous quarrel with Rimbaud, which brought him into prison for eighteen months, the accusation reads:

> "Pour avoir, à Bruxelles, le 10 juillet, 1873, volontairement portés des coups et fait des blessures ayant entraîné une incapacité de travail personnel à Arthur Rimbaud."

The whole account of this episode is given by M. Lepelletier in great detail, and from this we learn that it was by the merest change of mind on the part of Rimbaud, or by sudden treachery, that the matter came into the courts at all. Lepelletier supplies an unfavourable account of Rimbaud, whom he looks upon as the evil counsellor of Verlaine – probably with justice. There is little doubt that Rimbaud, apart from his genuine touch of precocious power, which had its influence on the genius of Verlaine, was a "mauvais sujet" of a selfish and mischievous kind. He was destructive and pitiless; and having done his worst, he went off carelessly into Africa.

It will surprise some readers to learn that Verlaine took his degree of "bachelier-ès-lettres," and that on leaving the Lycée Bonaparte he received a certificate placing him "au nombre des sujets distingués que compte l'établissement." He was well grounded in Latin, and fairly well in English, and at several intervals in his life attempted to master Spanish, with the vague desire of translating Calderon. At an early period he read French literature, classical and modern, with avidity; translations of English, German and Eastern classics; books of criticism and philosophy.

> "Il admirait beaucoup Joseph de Maîstre. *Le Rouge et le Noir* de Stendhal avait produce sur lui une forte impression. Il avait déniché, on ne sait où, une Vie de sainte Thérèse, qu'il lisait avec ravissement."

He was absorbed in Baudelaire, Gautier, Leconte de Lisle, Banville; he read Pétrus Borel and Aloysius Bertrand. The only poem that remains of this early period is the "Nocturne Parisien" of the *Poèmes Saturniens,* which dates from about his twentieth year. Jules de Goncourt defined it as "un beau poème sinistre mêlant comme une Morgue à Notre-Dame." Baudelaire, as Sainte-Beuve, in a charming letter of real appreciation, pointed out, is here the evident "point de départ, pour aller au delà."

The chapter in which Lepelletier tells the story of the origin of the most famous literary movement since that of 1830, the "Parnasse," is one of the most entertaining in the book, and gives, in its narrative of the receptions "chez Nina" (a *salon* which Lepelletier describes as the ancestor of the "Chat Noir"), a vivid picture of the days when Villiers de l'Isle-Adam and François Coppée were beginners together. Nina de Villars was one of the oddest people of her time: she made a kind of private Bohemia for poets, musicians, all kinds of artists and eccentric people, herself the most eccentric of them all. It was at her house that the members of the "Parnasse" gathered, while they selected as their more formal meeting-place the *salon* of Madame Ricard. It is not generally known that Verlaine's *Poèmes Saturniens* was the third volume to be issued by the house of Lemerre, afterwards to become a famous "publisher of poets," and it was in this volume that the new laws of the Parnasse were first formulated – that impassivity, that "marble egoism," which Verlaine was so soon to reject for a more living impulse, but which neither Leconte de Lisle nor Hérédia was ever to abandon. When one thinks of the later Verlaine, it is curious to turn to that first formula:

> Est-elle en marvre où non, le Vénus de Milo?

Verlaine's verse suddenly becomes human with *La Bonne Chanson,* though the humanity in it is not yet salted as with fire. It is the record of the event which, as Lepelletier says, dominated his whole life; the marriage with Mathilde Mauté, the young girl with whom he had fallen in love at first sight, and whose desertion of him, however explicable, he never forgot nor forgave. Nothing could be more just or delicate than Lepelletier's treatment of the whole situation and there is no doubt that he is right in saying that the young wife "eût une grande responsabilité dans les désordres de l'existence désorbitée du poète." Verlaine, as he says, "était bon, aimant, et c'était comme un souffrant qu'il fallait le traiter." "Vous n'avez rien compris à ma simplicité," he wrote long afterwards, addressing the woman of whom Lepelletier says, "Il l'aima toujours, il n'aima qu'elle."

With his marriage Verlaine's disasters begin. Rimbaud enters his life and turns the current of it; the vagabondage begins, in France and England, and the letters written from London are among the most vivid documents in the book: thumbnail sketches full of keen observation. Then comes his imprisonment and conversion to Catholicism. Here Lepelletier, while he gives us an infinity of details which he alone could give, adopts an attitude which we cannot think to be justified, and which, as a matter of fact, Verlaine protested against during his lifetime. "Cette conversion fut-elle profonde et véridique?" he asks; and he answers, "Je ne le crois pas." That his conversion had much influence on Verlaine's conduct cannot be contended, but conduct and belief are two different things. Sincerity of the moment was his fundamental characteristic, but the moments made and remade his moods in their passing. The religion of *Sagesse* is not the less genuine because that grave and sacred book was followed by the revolt of *Parallèment*. Verlaine tried to explain – in the poems themselves, in prefaces, and in conversation with friends – how natural it was to sin and to repent, and to use the same childlike words in the immediate rendering of sin and of repentance. This *naïveté*, which made any regular existence an impossibility, was a part of him which gave a quality to his work unlike that of any other poet of our time. At the end of his life hardly anything but the *naïveté* was left, and the poems became mere outcries and gestures. Lepelletier is justly indignant at the action of Vanier in publishing after Verlaine's deaths the collection called *Invectives*, made up of scraps and impromptus which the poet certainly never intended to publish. Here we see part of the weakness of a great man, who becomes petty when he puts off his true character and tries to be angry. "J'ai la fureur d'aimer," he says somewhere, and there is no essential part of his work which is not the expression of some form of love, grotesque or heroic, human or divine.

Of all this later, more and more miserable part of the life of

Verlaine, Lepelletier has less to tell us. It has been sufficiently commented on, not always by friendly or understanding witnesses. What we get in this book, for the first time, is a view of the life as a whole, with all that is beautiful, tragic, and desperate in it. It is not an apology: it is a statement. It not only does honor to a great and unhappy man of genius; it does him justice.

A NOTE ON PAUL VERLAINE

By Andrew Jary

Paul Verlaine (1844-1896) is one of the great 19th century French poets, part of the group that included Charles Baudelaire, Lautréamont, Gérard de Nerval and of course Arthur Rimbaud. Many of Verlaine's most significant poems are collected in this book, and Verlaine emerges as a highly accomplished artist, with a lyrical rhyming style that's wholly his own (and it sounds particularly beautiful in French – Verlaine is tricky to translate).

Paul Verlaine's era was that of Symbolism and Decadence, and the chief poets of Symbolism and Decadence included Verlaine, Charles Baudelaire, Arthur Rimbaud, Gérard de Nerval, Tristan Corbière, Stéphane Mallarmé, Paul Valéry and Lautréamont. The Symbolist and Decadent age is marked by 'gory exoticism', as Mario Praz put it (289), by the æstheticism of 'beauty', opulence and indulgence, mysticism and black magic, the macabre, where the key phrase is from Paul Verlaine: 'Je suis l'Empire à la fin de la décadence', which he wrote in 1885 in a poem entitled (what else?) 'Langueur'.[1] The word, *decadence*, from Verlaine, connotes profuse amounts of eroticism, debauchery, declining state power, Imperialism and 'perversions'.

Like other poets of the Symbolist era – Arthur Rimbaud,

---

1 P. Verlaine, 1999, 134.

Stéphane Mallarmé, Banville – Paul Verlaine can be seen as post-Romantic. Verlaine's poetry (like Symbolism) exhibits many affinities with Romanticism: the pantheism and nature mysticism; the love of occultism, paganism, Hellenism, travel and exotica; the cult of the individual; the social rebellion; the exaltation of solitude; the sense of melancholy; the emphasis on subjective experience; the use of drugs and intoxicants; the urge to go to extremes; the leaning towards infinity, and so on.

Paul Verlaine was an important poet, but was not epoch-forming like Arthur Rimbaud, Victor Hugo or Charles Baudelaire. Verlaine's poetry is marked by a finely-crafted musicality and sense of form, a delicate sensuality, and large doses of Catholic imagery and religious themes.

Paul Verlaine's emphasis in poetry on the form, precision, musicality and beauty of poetry contrasted dramatically with the sense of burning abandon in poets such as Rimbaud, de Nerval and Lautréamont. There is a wildness in Arthur Rimbaud's poetic sensibility that no poetic form can quite contain (despite his use of many traditional forms). While Verlaine's poetry remains firmly within the form of the stanza, Rimbaud's threatens to burst out. What Rimbaud and Verlaine share, with poets such as Baudelaire, William Blake, Novalis and Friedrich Hölderlin, is a belief in the magic of poetry. Theirs is a poetics of the word, an 'alchemy of the word'. as Rimbaud put it.

Paul Verlaine developed Gérard de Nerval's mythopoeic brand of poetry, but for Verlaine form was crucial. 'Music before everything', he wrote in his influential poem 'Art poétique' (1974, 172-3). Verlaine's delicate poetic musicality was highly refined even in his first volume of verse, *Poèmes saturniens*. A poem such as 'Cansons d'automne' displays the finesse of Verlaine's sense of sound and music in poetry (it's also an important poem for France politically):

> Les sanglots longs
> Des violons

    De l'automne
  Blessent mon cœur
  D'une langueur
    Monotone.

(The long sobbing of the violins of autumn wounds my heart with a monotonous languour [1974, 44])

VERLAINE AND RIMBAUD

It is significant that the main documents relating to the relationship between Paul Verlaine and Arthur Rimbaud is their poetry.[2] Poetry is a very particular kind of creation, often having an obscure or distant link to the poet's life or experience (involving layers and veils of stylization and mythicization). Consequently, using Verlaine's and Rimbaud's poems of the period or later poetry to find out about their years together is fraught with problems.

Paul Verlaine was ten years older than Arthur Rimbaud. Next to the phenomenally talented teenage poet, Verlaine must have felt inadequate. By an early age Rimbaud had already attained everything that Verlaine had, artistically, and had far surpassed him. The elements of their time together have become famous – the arguments, the dissolute life in Northern Europe (including Paris and London), and the incident with the gun, when Verlaine shot Rimbaud during an argument.

Before he met Paul Verlaine, Arthur Rimbaud admired his poetry. In his 'seer letter' of May 15, 1871, Rimbaud re-writes the history of poetry. It is all junk, he claims, from the Greeks to the Romantics (*Collected Works*, 305). Among the few poets to get a favourable mention by the young Rimbaud are the Parnassians Albert Mérat and Paul Verlaine (ib., 307).

---

2 W. Fowlie, 1995, 52.

Critics generally portray Paul Verlaine as the weaker, more feminine partner in their homosexual relationship, with Arthur Rimbaud as the more aggressive, more cynical partner. Rimbaud seemed to care much less about the relationship and about himself than Verlaine did. He certainly cared much less about art. It was Verlaine who tried to patch up the relationship after an interval apart. But both men had similar temperaments – too similar; both men were prone to violent mood swings; both were highly individual, self-opinionated, egotistic, unwilling to com-promise. They seemed well suited to each other, and yet, as events proved, ultimately incompatible.

Critics turn to Arthur Rimbaud's *A Season in Hell* (1873) as an account of aspects of the Verlaine-Rimbaud relationship: parts of *A Season In Hell* are intense, heartfelt, ashamed, vitriolic, un-repentant, transgressive, chaotic, stupid and sometimes violent. The first 'Delirium' poem is particularly visceral in its imagery, and intense in its self-examination.

Whether or not 'Delirium I: The Foolish Virgin' is an account of Arthur Rimbaud's time with Paul Verlaine, it certainly contains some of Rimbaud's most vivid and tortured poetry. Right from the start of 'Delirium I' the narrator or confessor is talking in extreme terms of being drunk, lost and impure. The confessor says that there has never been 'deliriums and tortures like this'. The confessor says he is really suffering. He speaks of the damned and the dead, of ghosts and murder, of treasure being stained with blood, of skeletons and throats being cut ('it'll be "disgusting"'). The Infernal Bridegroom says he will gash himself up, will make himself ugly, will howl in the streets: '[j]e veux devenir bien fou de rage (I want to become mad with rage)'.[3]

In 'Delirium I', Arthur Rimbaud's poetic voice apparently impersonates that of a 'Foolish Virgin' (taken to be Paul Verlaine) discussing her 'Infernal Bridegroom' (taken to be Rimbaud). However, before the reader accepts 'Delirium I' as a record of the

---

3 A. Rimbaud, *Complete Works*, 188, tr. A. Jary.

French poets' famous, gay love affair, it is worth recalling that poetic accounts of people's lives can be distortions, exagger-ations, or complete pretense. The reality of the life Verlaine and Rimbaud led may hardly appear in *A Season in Hell*, or in any of Rimbaud's poetry. Poets alter life in their poems as they wish – for artistic reasons, or for any number of motives. It is problematic working back from the poems to the poet's life: this is demonstrated by considering William Shakespeare's *Sonnets* and how they relate to the 'real' Shakespeare's relationship with the beloved youth and the 'Dark Lady', or when considering the 'real' Francesco Petrarch's relationship with the 'real' Laura de Sade, the subject of Petrarch's *Canzoniere*.

Remember, then, that in 'Delirium I: The Foolish Virgin' in *A Season in Hell*, a very clever and self-aware poet (Arthur Rimbaud) is impersonating a strange character called the 'Foolish Virgin' which may relate to Paul Verlaine. Also, if the reader swops the roles of the 'Foolish Virgin' and the 'Infernal Bride-groom', the poem is equally insightful. Even if this is biography or autobiography, it is a very peculiar kind of biography or auto-biography. Poems are seldom as straightforward as biographies (or novels) anyway; poems are distinct forms of expression with their own laws and needs. Rimbaud's poems, in particular, are highly idiosyncratic. Given the kind of poet that Rimbaud was, the kind of poems that he wrote, his personal aesthetics, his intense self-awareness (in life as in poetry), and his unique life-philosophy, one should not automatically see texts such as 'Delirium I' as biography.

Paul Verlaine also poeticized Arthur Rimbaud – most famously in poem 'À Arthur Rimbaud':

> Mortel, ange ET démon, autaunt dire Rimbaud,
> Tu mérites la prime place en ce mien livre,
> Bien que tel sot grimaud t'ait traité de ribaud
> Imberbe et de monstre en herbe et de potache ivre.

The poems of Paul Verlaine re-pay any visit, as the poems

selected for this book demonstrate. Verlaine is a poet who carved out his own niche in the history of poetry: his poems are instantly recognizable for their imagery and themes, and perhaps for their pure poetic approach, more than anything. Verlaine is a 'poet's poet'.

BIBLIOGRAPHY

BY PAUL VERLAINE

Forty Poems, tr. R. Gant & C. Apcher, Falcon Press, 1948
Œuvres poétiques complètes, ed. Y.-G. Le Dantec, Gallimard, 1951
The Sky Above the Roof, tr. B. Hill, Rupert Hart-Davis, 1957
Odeds en Son Honneur Élégies, Librairie Armand Colin, Paris, 1959
Selected Poems, tr. Joanna Richardson, Penguin, London, 1974
Fêtes galantes, ed. Jean Gaudon, Garnier-Flammarion, 1976
Femmes, Hombres, tr. A. Elliot, Anvil Press, London, 1979
One Hundred and One Poems, tr. N. Shapiro, University Press, Chicago, IL, 1999

ABOUT PAUL VERLANIE

E. Delahaye. *Rimbaud*, Messein, 1928
—. *Souveniers familiers à propos de Rimbaud, Verlaine et Germain Nouveau*, Messein, 1925
W. Fowlie. *Rimbaud*, University of Chicago Press, Chicago, 1965
—. *Rimbaud and Jim Morrison: The Rebel as Poet*, Souvenir, 1995
C.A. Hackett. *Rimbaud*, Hilary House, New York, NY, 1977
—. "Verlaine's Influence on Rimbaud", in Lloyd James Austin, ed. *Studies in Modern French Literature Presented to P. Mansell Jones*, Manchester University Press, Manchester, 1961, 163-180
J. & V. Hanson. *Verlaine, Prince of Poets*, Chatto & Windus, London, 1959
Mario Praz: *The Romantic Agony*, tr. A. Davidson, Oxford University Press, Oxford, 1933
Joanna Richardson. *Verlaine*, Weidenfeld & Nicolson, London, 1971
P. Schmidt. "Visions of Violence: Rimbaud and Verlaine", in G.

Stambolian, 228-242

George Stambolian & Elaine Marks, eds. *Homosexuality and French Literature: Cultural Contexts/ Critical Texts*, Cornell University Press, Ithaca, 1979

V.P. Underwood. *Verlaine et l'Angleterre*, Nizet, 1956

BY ARTHUR RIMBAUD

Œuvres, ed. Suzanne Bernard & André Guyaux, Garnier, 1981
Œuvres complètes, ed. Antoine Adam, Gallimard, 1972
Complete Works, Selected Letters, tr. Wallace Fowlie, University of Chicago Press, Chicago, 1966
Collected Poems, ed. Oliver Bernhard, Penguin, London, 1986
Illuminations, tr. Louise Varèse, New Directions, New York, NY, 1946
A Season In Hell, tr. Andrew Jary, Crescent Moon, 2007
Morning of Ecstasy: Selected Poems, tr. Andrew Jary, Crescent Moon, 2007

Arseny Tarkovsky

Selected Poems

Arseny Tarkovsky is the neglected Russian poet, father of the acclaimed film director Andrei Tarkovsky. This new book gathers together many of Tarkovsky's most lyrical and heartfelt poems, in Virginia Rounding's new, clear translations. Many of Tarkovsky's poems appeared in his son's films, such as *Mirror*, *Stalker*, *Nostalghia* and *The Sacrifice*. There is an introduction by Rounding, and a bibliography of both Arseny and Andrei Tarkovsky.

Illustrated. Bibliography and notes.
ISBN 9781816171144 Pbk   ISBN 9781861712660 Hbk

Beauties, Beasts, and Enchantment

CLASSIC FRENCH FAIRY TALES

Translated and with an Introduction
by Jack Zipes

A collection of 36 classic French fairy tales translated by renowned writer Jack Zipes. *Cinderella*, *Beauty and the Beast*, *Sleeping Beauty* and *Little Red Riding Hood* are among the classic fairy tales in this amazing book.
Includes illustrations from fairy tale collections.
Jack Zipes has written and published widely on fairy tales.

'Terrific... a succulent array of 17th and 18th century 'salon' fairy tales'
- *The New York Times Book Review*

'These tales are adventurous, thrilling in a way fairy tales are meant to be... The translation from the French is modern, happily free of archaic and hyperbolic language... a fine and sophisticated collection' - *New York Tribune*

'Enjoyable to read... a unique collection of French regional folklore' - *Library Journal*

'Charming stories accompanied by attractive pen-and-ink drawings' - *Chattanooga Times*

Introduction and illustrations   612pp.   ISBN 9781861712510 Pbk   ISBN 9781861713193 Hbk

In the Dim Void

Samuel Beckett's Late Trilogy: *Company, Ill Seen, Ill Said* and *Worstward Ho*

by Gregory Johns

This book discusses the luminous beauty and dense, rigorous poetry of Samuel Beckett's late works, *Company, Ill Seen, Ill Said* and *Worstward Ho*. Gregory Johns looks back over Beckett's long writing career, charting the development from the *Molloy-Malone Dies-Unnamable* trilogy through the 'fizzles' of the 1960s to the elegiac lyricism of the *Company* series. Johns compares the trilogy with late plays such as *Ghosts*, *Footfalls* and *Rockaby*.

Bibliography, notes. Illustrated. 120pp
ISBN 9781861712974 Pbk and ISBN 9781861712608 Hbk
9781861713407 E-book

CRESCENT MOON PUBLISHING

web: www.crmoon.com e-mail: cresmopub@yahoo.co.uk

ARTS, PAINTING, SCULPTURE

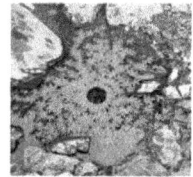

The Art of Andy Goldsworthy
Andy Goldsworthy: Touching Nature
Andy Goldsworthy in Close-Up
Andy Goldsworthy: Pocket Guide
Andy Goldsworthy In America
Land Art: A Complete Guide
The Art of Richard Long
Richard Long: Pocket Guide
Land Art In the UK
Land Art in Close-Up
Land Art In the U.S.A.
Land Art: Pocket Guide
Installation Art in Close-Up
Minimal Art and Artists In the 1960s and After
Colourfield Painting
Land Art DVD, TV documentary
Andy Goldsworthy DVD, TV documentary
The Erotic Object: Sexuality in Sculpture From Prehistory to the Present Day
Sex in Art: Pornography and Pleasure in Painting and Sculpture
Postwar Art
Sacred Gardens: The Garden in Myth, Religion and Art
Glorification: Religious Abstraction in Renaissance and 20th Century Art

Early Netherlandish Painting
Leonardo da Vinci
Piero della Francesca
Giovanni Bellini
Fra Angelico: Art and Religion in the Renaissance
Mark Rothko: The Art of Transcendence
Frank Stella: American Abstract Artist
Jasper Johns
Brice Marden
Alison Wilding: The Embrace of Sculpture
Vincent van Gogh: Visionary Landscapes
Eric Gill: Nuptials of God
Constantin Brancusi: Sculpting the Essence of Things
Max Beckmann
Caravaggio
Gustave Moreau
Egon Schiele: Sex and Death In Purple Stockings
Delizioso Fotografico Fervore: Works In Process 1
Sacro Cuore: Works In Process 2
The Light Eternal: J.M.W. Turner
The Madonna Glorified: Karen Arthurs

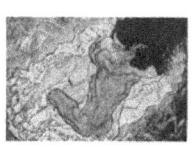

LITERATURE

J.R.R. Tolkien: The Books, The Films, The Whole Cultural Phenomenon
J.R.R. Tolkien: Pocket Guide
Tolkien's Heroic Quest
The *Earthsea* Books of Ursula Le Guin
Beauties, Beasts and Enchantment: Classic French Fairy Tales
German Popular Stories by the Brothers Grimm
Philip Pullman and *His Dark Materials*
Sexing Hardy: Thomas Hardy and Feminism
Thomas Hardy's *Tess of the d'Urbervilles*
Thomas Hardy's *Jude the Obscure*
Thomas Hardy: The Tragic Novels
Love and Tragedy: Thomas Hardy
The Poetry of Landscape in Hardy
Wessex Revisited: Thomas Hardy and John Cowper Powys
Wolfgang Iser: Essays and Interviews
Petrarch, Dante and the Troubadours
Maurice Sendak and the Art of Children's Book Illustration
Andrea Dworkin
Cixous, Irigaray, Kristeva: The *Jouissance* of French Feminism
Julia Kristeva: Art, Love, Melancholy, Philosophy, Semiotics and Psychoanalysis
Hélene Cixous I Love You: The *Jouissance* of Writing
Luce Irigaray: Lips, Kissing, and the Politics of Sexual Difference
Peter Redgrove: Here Comes the Flood
Peter Redgrove: Sex-Magic-Poetry-Cornwall
Lawrence Durrell: Between Love and Death, East and West
Love, Culture & Poetry: Lawrence Durrell
Cavafy: Anatomy of a Soul
German Romantic Poetry: Goethe, Novalis, Heine, Hölderlin
Feminism and Shakespeare
Shakespeare: Love, Poetry & Magic
The Passion of D.H. Lawrence
D.H. Lawrence: Symbolic Landscapes
D.H. Lawrence: Infinite Sensual Violence
Rimbaud: Arthur Rimbaud and the Magic of Poetry
The Ecstasies of John Cowper Powys
Sensualism and Mythology: The Wessex Novels of John Cowper Powys
Amorous Life: John Cowper Powys and the Manifestation of Affectivity (H.W. Fawkner)
Postmodern Powys: New Essays on John Cowper Powys (Joe Boulter)
Rethinking Powys: Critical Essays on John Cowper Powys
Paul Bowles & Bernardo Bertolucci
Rainer Maria Rilke
Joseph Conrad: *Heart of Darkness*
In the Dim Void: Samuel Beckett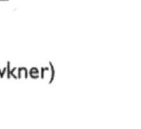
Samuel Beckett Goes into the Silence
André Gide: Fiction and Fervour
Jackie Collins and the Blockbuster Novel
Blinded By Her Light: The Love-Poetry of Robert Graves
The Passion of Colours: Travels In Mediterranean Lands
Poetic Forms

POETRY

Ursula Le Guin: Walking In Cornwall
Peter Redgrove: Here Comes The Flood
Peter Redgrove: Sex-Magic-Poetry-Cornwall
Dante: Selections From the Vita Nuova
Petrarch, Dante and the Troubadours
William Shakespeare: Sonnets
William Shakespeare: Complete Poems
Blinded By Her Light: The Love-Poetry of Robert Graves
Emily Dickinson: Selected Poems
Emily Brontë: Poems
Thomas Hardy: Selected Poems
Percy Bysshe Shelley: Poems
John Keats: Selected Poems
Joh n Keats: Poems of 1820
D.H. Lawrence: Selected Poems
Edmund Spenser: Poems
Edmund Spenser: Amoretti
John Donne: Poems
Henry Vaughan: Poems
Sir Thomas Wyatt: Poems
Robert Herrick: Selected Poems
Rilke: Space, Essence and Angels in the Poetry of Rainer Maria Rilke
Rainer Maria Rilke: Selected Poems
Friedrich Hölderlin: Selected Poems
Arseny Tarkovsky: Selected Poems
Arthur Rimbaud: Selected Poems
Arthur Rimbaud: A Season in Hell
Arthur Rimbaud and the Magic of Poetry
Novalis: Hymns To the Night
German Romantic Poetry
Paul Verlaine: Selected Poems
Elizaethan Sonnet Cycles
D.J. Enright: By-Blows
Jeremy Reed: Brigitte's Blue Heart
Jeremy Reed: Claudia Schiffer's Red Shoes
Gorgeous Little Orpheus
Radiance: New Poems
Crescent Moon Book of Nature Poetry
Crescent Moon Book of Love Poetry
Crescent Moon Book of Mystical Poetry
Crescent Moon Book of Elizabethan Love Poetry
Crescent Moon Book of Metaphysical Poetry
Crescent Moon Book of Romantic Poetry
Pagan America: New American Poetry

MEDIA, CINEMA, FEMINISM and CULTURAL STUDIES

J.R.R. Tolkien: The Books, The Films, The Whole Cultural Phenomenon
J.R.R. Tolkien: Pocket Guide
The *Lord of the Rings* Movies: Pocket Guide
The Cinema of Hayao Miyazaki
Hayao Miyazaki: *Princess Mononoke*: Pocket Movie Guide
Hayao Miyazaki: *Spirited Away*: Pocket Movie Guide
Tim Burton : Hallowe'en For Hollywood
Ken Russell
Ken Russell: *Tommy*: Pocket Movie Guide
The Ghost Dance: The Origins of Religion
The Peyote Cult
Cixous, Irigaray, Kristeva: The *Jouissance* of French Feminism
Julia Kristeva: Art, Love, Melancholy, Philosophy, Semiotics and Psychoanalysis
Luce Irigaray: Lips, Kissing, and the Politics of Sexual Difference
Hélène Cixous I Love You: The *Jouissance* of Writing
Andrea Dworkin
'Cosmo Woman': The World of Women's Magazines
Women in Pop Music
HomeGround: The Kate Bush Anthology
Discovering the Goddess (Geoffrey Ashe)
The Poetry of Cinema
The Sacred Cinema of Andrei Tarkovsky
Andrei Tarkovsky: Pocket Guide
Andrei Tarkovsky: *Mirror*: Pocket Movie Guide
Andrei Tarkovsky: *The Sacrifice*: Pocket Movie Guide
Walerian Borowczyk: Cinema of Erotic Dreams
Jean-Luc Godard: The Passion of Cinema
Jean-Luc Godard: *Hail Mary*: Pocket Movie Guide
Jean-Luc Godard: *Contempt*: Pocket Movie Guide
Jean-Luc Godard: *Pierrot le Fou*: Pocket Movie Guide
John Hughes and Eighties Cinema
Ferris Bueller's Day Off: Pocket Movie Guide
Jean-Luc Godard: Pocket Guide
The Cinema of Richard Linklater
Liv Tyler: Star In Ascendance
Blade Runner and the Films of Philip K. Dick
Paul Bowles and Bernardo Bertolucci
Media Hell: Radio, TV and the Press
An Open Letter to the BBC
Detonation Britain: Nuclear War in the UK
Feminism and Shakespeare
Wild Zones: Pornography, Art and Feminism
Sex in Art: Pornography and Pleasure in Painting and Sculpture
Sexing Hardy: Thomas Hardy and Feminism

The Light Eternal is a model monograph, an exemplary job. The subject matter of the book is beautifully organised and dead on beam. (Lawrence Durrell)

It is amazing for me to see my work treated with such passion and respect. (Andrea Dworkin)

CRESCENT MOON PUBLISHING
P.O. Box 1312, Maidstone, Kent, ME14 5XU, Great Britain. www.crmoon.com

cresmopub@yahoo.co.uk   www.crescentmoon.org.uk

www.ingramcontent.com/pod-product-compliance
Lightning Source LLC
Chambersburg PA
CBHW070155100426
42743CB00013B/2915